What they said about *Minute Family*:

"This is no ordinary self-help manual. Elegantly and compellingly written, with both sensitivity and humour, it offers an insight into the everyday challenges experienced by real-life families and of how they can be overcome."
Ned Temko, *The Observer*

"With wit and insight Rob Parsons gets to the heart of what makes families work – time, attention and encouragement... too many families are destroyed by parents simply not making their children and their partners their main priority. Parsons shows you how to do so, by listening, communicating, and having fun. Reading this may be the best 60 minutes you will ever spend."
Suzie Hayman, BBC radio agony aunt and author of *Teach Yourself Parenting Your Teenager*

"I would recommend this book to anyone, whatever their family circumstance, as it's a book of encouragement and a challenge to look beyond our own experience to the needs of those family members who surround us."
Jeremy Todd, Chief Executive, Parentline Plus

"In the twenty-first century, we're overwhelmed with knowledge and good advice but perhaps a bit short on wisdom and honesty. Rob Parsons redresses that balance in his excellent and very readable book, any page of which could revolutionize your family life and your children's futures. That must be worth at least 60 minutes of anyone's time, however busy we think we are!"
Ken Shorey, Chief Executive, Positive Parenting

"Follow some of the ideas in this book and you will be top of the pops with your children! The ultimate gift to our families is our time."
Duncan Fisher OBE, 'Kids in the Middle'

"Comforting, profound and wonderfully *real* – it will touch the heart of *your* family."
Katharine Hill, author of *Rules of Engagement*

"I found this an inspiring, sensible and easy to follow book offering practical guidelines. It would make a great read for any family... I believe this book could revitalize any family and make good ones even better."
Dave Lumsdon, Senior Educational Psychologist, Northumberland County Council & Newcastle University

"With great warmth and wisdom, Rob Parsons has done an invaluable service showing modern day families how to not to suffer from the time-crunch – and how to prioritize what's really important in all our lives."
Tanith Carey, author of *How to Be an Amazing Mum When You Just Don't Have the Time*

"This book is a 'must' for all families. It is down to earth, comforting, and wonderfully real."
Rachel Waddilove, author of *The Baby Book*

What they said about Rob Parsons and his books:

"The man who reinvented Fatherhood."
Linda Lee Potter, *The Daily Mail*

"Rob Parsons is one of the most inspirational speakers in the country today... motivating, practical and giving you the sense that somebody has just turned the light on."
Rosemary Conley, Chairman, The Rosemary Conley Group

"Parsons is unlike any other business gurus... he identifies an emerging social class – the new poor."
Des Dearlove, *The Times*

"Rob Parsons has an uncanny ability for asking some of life's most challenging questions in an unobtrusive way."
Jill Garrett, former Managing Director, The Gallup Organisation UK

THE
Sixty
MINUTE
Family

This is a "Sixty Minute"
book, which means that
if you are quick, you can
read it in an hour. An hour?
What can be said of value
that can be read in less
than 4,000 seconds?
Well, *something* at least…

A Lion Book
an imprint of
Lion Hudson plc
Wilkinson House, Jordan Hill Road,
Oxford OX2 8DR, England
www.lionhudson.com

ISBN 978 0 7459 5383 0

Distributed by:
UK: Marston Book Services, PO Box 269, Abingdon, Oxon, OX14 4YN
USA: Trafalgar Square Publishing, 814 N. Franklin Street, Chicago, IL 60610
USA Christian Market: Kregel Publications, PO Box 2607, Grand Rapids, MI 49501

First edition 2010
10 9 8 7 6 5 4 3 2 1 0

Acknowledgments
p. 93: Extract from George Bernard Shaw, *Man and Superman*; The Society of Authors
on behalf of the Bernard Shaw Estate.

This book has been printed on paper and board independently certified
as having been produced from sustainable forests.

A catalogue record for this book is available
from the British Library

Typeset in 10/14.5 ITC Stone Serif
Printed and bound in Great Britain by J F Print Ltd., Sparkford, Somerset.

THE
Sixty
MINUTE
Family

An hour to
transform
your relationships
– forever

Rob Parsons

LION

To Dianne, Kate, Paul, Lloyd, Becky and Ron –
thank you.

Contents

Acknowledgments

Sheron Rice simply made it a better book – again! Eddie Bell, my agent, of the Bell Lomax Moreton agency, is brilliant – I am so grateful to him and his colleagues Pat, Paul, and June for all their wisdom and support. My thanks also go to Kate Kirkpatrick and the team at Lion Hudson. The Care for the Family staff have done their usual wonderful job and so many others have as well, including Naomi Buckler, Paul Francis, Kate Hancock, Katharine Hill, John Gallacher, David Lumsdon, Jon and Sarah Mason, Mark Molden, and Steve Williams.

The Hospital Waiting Room

It is midnight. I am in the waiting room of my local hospital. I've brought a neighbour in because he's had a fall, and I've now been sitting for over four hours on plastic chairs that were designed to cause as much discomfort as possible to every part of my anatomy.

I get up, stretch my legs, and wander across to the coffee machine. A young woman of perhaps twenty-four years old is there. She is obviously distraught and drops the coins she is trying to feed into the machine. I suggest she take a seat, I pick up the money, and get her coffee for her.

We start chatting and she tells me that her father is seriously ill, and there is some doubt that he will make it through the night. As we sip our drinks, I ask her to tell me about him.

She brushes a tear from her face, smiles, and says, "My mum and dad were brilliant – our family life was wonderful. I didn't know how good it was until I went to college and heard my friends talk about how life was in their homes. It wasn't that we didn't argue – we did, lots of times. We were all so very different. I was the rebellious one. I have two sisters and a brother. Sometimes we'd practically come to blows. But we laughed a lot and always knew in our hearts that when it came down to it, we'd be there for each other."

I say, "It sounds like a great family."

She nods. "Dad was from a poor home, but he did really well in his career. In fact, in the early years of my parents' marriage he put in such long hours at his office they nearly broke up. After that he changed. It wasn't that he didn't continue to work hard, but unlike previously, he was always there when we needed him. I'd be in a school play and suddenly I'd see him slip in at the back. He was sometimes a little late, but he hated missing any of that stuff; it was the same with my brother's football matches. After he and Mum went through that hard time, it seemed his priorities changed."

I ask, "Is your mum still alive?"

"Oh yes," she says. "She's up in the ward with him now..."

I say, "Tell me more..."

It was after two in the morning when we stopped talking, and it had all been about her family life. She told me of holidays and Christmases, of good times and harder ones, and of conflicts that were finally resolved with tears and forgiveness. She spoke of silly things they'd done – like giving each other names from the *Jungle Book* film for a whole week. She said, "The only problem with that was that we were all teenagers!"

She said, "My mother always used to say the same thing whenever we'd done something silly together, or scary (like when we went abseiling once and my sister got stuck upside down), or even when we'd come through a tough time. She would say, 'We made a memory.'"

She swallowed hard and I said, "You have lots of them, don't you?"

"Yes," she said. "I have hundreds." She smiled. "Well, I'd better go back up to the ward now. Thanks for talking to me. It helped."

I eventually left the hospital at 9 a.m. As I was approaching my car, I noticed a young couple in the parking bay next to mine. They were gingerly loading an obviously brand-new baby into their vehicle, together with various bouquets of flowers. I shouted, "Congratulations!" The father smiled at me.

As I got into my car, I found myself thinking of the young woman at the coffee machine and wishing that her father could have shared some of the lessons he'd learned with these new parents at the start of their family life together. And as I let my mind wander, I felt I could almost hear the older man talk of things that make families strong: the need to make time for each other; the power of laughter; the creating of homes where forgiveness is always on the heels of conflict; and how to make a memory.

For over twenty years I have travelled the world and listened to people tell me the stories of their families. From Moscow to Melbourne, from Durban to Doncaster, they have shared with me what made their families strong – and sometimes what destroyed them.

My own children are now at the start of their own family life. If they let me – a big if! – what lessons would I love to share with them? Perhaps things I wish I'd done differently – what seemed to work and what didn't. But these are not just my lessons – they are gleaned from talking to families across the world, sometimes listening to people who often said, "I wish I'd known that earlier in my family life." So, whether my children ever read them or not – and acknowledging that somebody else's list may be quite different – here, at least, are my ten life lessons for a strong family life.

This is a "Sixty Minute" book, which means that if you are quick, you can read it in an hour. An hour? What can be said of value that can be read in less than 4,000 seconds? Well, *something* at least... And I know this: whatever size and shape your family is – mother and father, single parent mum or dad, stepfamily – this short book contains things that have the potential to make your family stronger and perhaps even save it from breakup. I've known families whose relationships were changed, saved even, by putting into practice just one of the lessons in this book.

If, at the moment, you are going through a good time in your family life, I hope these lessons will make it even better. However, you may be going through a difficult period right now. In my work I see too much of real life to believe there are easy answers to the problems of families in pain. But I hope you will still find something that will help – even if it's simply the realization that whatever you are experiencing, you are not alone.

So where do we begin? We begin with a life lesson that the father of the girl I met at the hospital grasped in time to make a difference in his family. It may seem simple, but it is vital. Miss this life lesson and no matter how well we look after those we love materially, we'll find it hard to build a strong family. For in many ways, success in all the other lessons is dependent on how far we manage to achieve success in this, the first.

To Make Time for My Family

I wanted a boy first. I *believed* we would have a boy first. My wife, Dianne, was having a Caesarean section, and in those far off days they didn't let fathers within 50 metres of the operating theatre, never mind gown you up and allow you to shout helpful hints to the surgeon. I waited in the corridor outside and finally a nurse came out and said, "You've got a lovely daughter." I smiled, but my heart fell. And then they brought Katie out in a little cot and suddenly another woman walked into my life and I fell in love all over again. I knew at that moment that I was forever smitten. I had a family. I would care for this family, I would provide for it, and, if necessary, I would give my life for it.

So why was it so very hard to give them my *time*?

Priorities

As I write, Captain Chesley Sullenberger has just crash-landed a US Airways Airbus on the Hudson River. Because of his skill, there were no fatalities and yet the passengers on that plane did not know they would escape death as they took the brace position on that icy winter's morning. And because they didn't know the outcome, they did what people do when they think they might die: they use what little time they think they have left to tell those nearest to them how precious they are. One woman told her story, but it could have been multiplied many times over. She said, "As soon as I knew we were in trouble I rang my family on my cell phone to say, 'I love you.'"

So here's the dilemma: if family life is so important to us, why, so often, do we fail to give enough time to those we love most?

To find the answer, go back to that plane hurtling at over 100 mph towards the Hudson River. Its passengers believed with all their hearts that time was limited – perhaps to just a few minutes. In those circumstances, they had to decide how to use that time. They had to ask, "What are my priorities?"

They could have chosen to ring clients or customers, the garage about the new car, or perhaps a colleague to put the final touches to that presentation for the meeting tomorrow. But they didn't. They did what men and women the world over do when they know that time is short: they chose to give the time to their families.

I know what some of you are thinking. You're saying to yourselves, "But that's an extreme situation. Anybody would choose family if they knew their time was limited." But the truth is that our time *is* limited – we simply don't realize it.

Families that don't have time for each other don't *intend* to live that way. It's just that life goes by a day at a time, and because there's always tomorrow, the problem never seems critical. The people on the plane that day thought there may not be a tomorrow for them, but in our everyday family life we believe the opposite: that there will *always* be tomorrow.

Our child says, "Dad, can we build that den you promised me?" and we say, "We'll do it later, Son." The only problem is that one day when we do have time to make a house out of bits of wood, he's got other plans. Or perhaps he's a teenager now and doesn't want to be seen within 5 miles of us. What a tragedy. Just at the moment when we have time for our children, they've learned to say, "Great idea, Dad. But would you mind if we did it later?"

When my son, Lloyd, was a young child he'd always come into the bathroom at about 7:30 a.m. when I was shaving and say, "Tell me a story, Dad." It was often the last thing I felt like doing – my head would already be spinning with what the day ahead might hold – but usually I managed to stumble out some tale of the school bully who picked on the karate expert by mistake.

I told those stories week in, week out, and down the years. Then one morning as I was putting away my razor and soap, I realized that Lloyd hadn't come in for his story. I yelled downstairs, "Hey, Lloyd, do you want a quick story?" He shouted back, "No thanks, Dad – I'm playing with Kate. Tell me one tomorrow." I'm sure I told Lloyd stories on other occasions in his young life, but there never was another "shaving tale". I wish he'd warned me on that cold November morning that it was the last time we'd do it: I would have made more of it.

But don't start feeling guilty about all of this. We have to live in the real world. There will be some nights when we're absolutely shattered, and it's fine to skip pages when we're reading stories to them. (The trouble is, though, that kids are too clever: "Silly Daddy," she says, "you've missed forty-nine pages.") But at the same time, it's as well to remember how fast those doors of childhood close.

Over the past twenty years, especially since writing *The Heart of Success*, I have spoken to thousands of people about their lives at work. Some have achieved more than they'd ever thought possible, but as they've shared the story of their success, it's evident that they've paid an enormous price for it. Sometimes, as they're approaching retirement, they say: "I've achieved all this, but where did my life go?"

The truth is that whether we're a bank clerk, a doctor, or a firefighter, life is busy. We have to put bread on the table. We can't always give our families all the time we would like to. Nevertheless, if we're to have a hope of giving our family as much time as we can, there are some "Time Myths" we have to deal with.

Myth Number 1:
It's All a Matter of Organization

We sometimes read in the press of people who say that balancing the demands of work and family life is simply a matter of organization. They seem to be able to run high-powered careers, sit on the boards of various charitable organizations, read stories to their kids each night, and bake cakes that would make Jamie Oliver want to take cooking lessons.

But it's not just a matter of organization. The truth is that every choice we make as to how we use our time precludes another choice that we might have made. The old saying is true: "If you do *this*, you can't do *that*." Simply put, the idea that you can have it all *and* do it all is an illusion. Supermum or Superdad is not out there. You can wear your underwear outside your trousers, but you still can't fly.

Myth Number 2:
One Day We'll Have More Time

I've had hundreds of conversations, particularly with men, during which they've said something like this to me: "We got married and I worked hard to give my family the best I could. I did well in my job. I didn't have much time for my family, but I believed that would come later. We've enjoyed a reasonable lifestyle – perhaps a very good one. Now I'm fifty and I want to spend time with my children, but the truth is they really don't want to know. It's not that they don't love me; it's just that *their* lives are busy now. It seems that my children, and even my partner, have learned to live without me. In some ways I feel cheated."

Of course, this lifestyle is not often one that is chosen deliberately. It is rather that we live it, promising ourselves that we'll have more time one day. We say, "Next week will be a little quieter..." or "When I get promoted/when the exams are over/when this big job is out of the way/ when I've finished decorating the living room/when I move to the new office... I'll have more time for the family." If you take nothing else of value from this short book, at least take this: a slower day is not coming. If you have anything that matters to you, try to give some time to it – *today*.

Myth Number 3:
We Have to Work Long Hours to Give Our Kids the Best

Most of us want to provide for our children as well as we possibly can. But we should be careful. Someone has summed up the pitfall well: "We are so busy giving our kids what we *didn't* have, we don't have time to give them what we *did* have."

But even when we've dealt with the myths, finding that time is still not easy...

The Time Supermarket

A vast supermarket opens up in your area, but instead of food and drink it sells ways you can spend your life. Instead of money, the currency is *time*. And instead of Bakery, Meat, and Fruit and Veg, the departments in the store are Jobs and Careers, Hobbies, Television and Audio, Social Life, Sleeping, Eating, Personal Hygiene, and Family.

On the day your first child is born, you are invited to the store. The supermarket manager takes you into his office and tells you the rules: "Each week you must come to the store to spend your time. You are allocated the same amount of time that is given to every person, rich or poor: 168 hours per week."

"That sounds a lot," you say. "What if I don't spend it all?"

The manager smiles. "There's never been a person in the history of the world who did *not* spend it all."

You shrug your shoulders: "OK. How does it work?"

"Well," says the manager, "there are some things you *have* to buy. We suggest you spend eight hours a day on sleep, another eight on work, an hour on travel, two hours on eating, and thirty minutes on personal hygiene."

The manager sees us frowning as we try to do the maths in our head. "Let me save you the bother," he says. "On a weekday, you'll have four and half hours left to spend in other sections."

"That doesn't seem much," you mutter, pushing your trolley into the store.

One day as you leave the store, sad-faced, an old man strikes up a conversation with you. "Why so glum?" he says.

"Oh," you say. "I love my wife and my kids, but by the time I get to the Family department, I've spent all my time – there just isn't enough to go around."

The old man smiles and says, "Let me give you a couple of tips…"

Some months later the manager stops you. "You've got me puzzled," he says.

You smile. "Really?"

"Yes," he says. "When you come in to shop these days, you're taking a different route around the departments. After you've been to the Sleep section, Jobs and Careers, Personal Hygiene, and Eating, you go directly to an aisle at the back, passing straight by our wonderful offerings in Television and Audio, Hobbies, and even Social Life. Why do you do that?"

"Well," you say. "It's because that's where the Family department is. I usually buy some story time with my two-year-old and some playtime with my six-year-old. And I also buy enough time to watch my daughter's hockey match and usually enough for an evening a week with my wife."

The manager looks puzzled. "But why do you go there first?"

"Oh, that's easy," you say. "At first I always *intended* to buy things from the Family department, but by the time I got there, I'd spent all of my time – one week I spent twenty hours on Television and Audio alone! And then somebody told me that because time is limited, it is vital to put the most important things in the trolley first."

"I see," the manager says. "But I've noticed something else, as well. You always used to park your car then rush straight into the store, but now you sit in it writing for a while before you come in. What are you doing?"

"Well, it's simply this," you say. "For a few weeks – even after I realized I needed to go to the Family section first – I still found that I'd often get distracted by other departments on my way there. And I'd end up still running out of time for the family… until I made a list. Now, before I go into the store, I sit in my car and I *plan* what I'm going to get."

"I love it when a plan comes together."
– Colonel "Hannibal" Smith, *The A-Team*

Resolving to enjoy family life together is one thing, but how do we actually *make it happen*? Why is it that some families seem to have so much more time than others? Is it that other people have less demanding jobs or earn enough money to pay others to look after the everyday things? Well, sometimes – but certainly not always. No, the simple secret of families that have time for each other is that they've made it a priority – they actually *plan* for it.

It's not enough to *want* to go to your daughter's school play – life is busy, and a hundred things will conspire to keep you from it. In fact, *wanting* to go won't get you within 10 miles of *The Wizard of Oz*. No, if you are to achieve this goal, you'll have to *believe* it is a priority – that this event is important. You'll have to believe it matters that a daughter sees her mother or father in the audience. If you do believe it, you will often turn up even when you don't really want to – let's face it, plenty of the stuff we do with kids is not exactly riveting.

But even believing it's a priority will not be enough to get you there. You have to take a second step and *plan to be there*. That means taking it seriously. It means sitting down with a calendar at the beginning of a school term and writing in the important dates.

American television used to run an advert which showed a small girl approaching her father as he was doing some office work at home. He was busily entering appointments into his planner. She said, "Dad, what are you doing?" He didn't look up from his task, just mumbled, "I'm putting in times when I can see some really important people." She said, "Dad, am I in that book?"

Action Points

Make a family calendar and block out an evening per week right now for "family time" with the emphasis on fun – playing board games, watching a DVD and eating popcorn, making a photo collage, or sleeping in the living room and telling stories by torchlight.

Spend ten minutes with your kids doing the fun "How well do you know your child?" online quiz at www.careforthefamily.org.uk/knowyourchild.

Does finding time seem impossible? If so, what could you STOP doing so that you can START doing something else?

Have a regular "date night" with your husband or wife. It needn't be expensive, but make sure the mobile phone's switched off.

If it's possible, take your child to the place where you work. Let them sit in your seat or stand at the bench where you work.

Put important dates into your diary now – school concerts, football matches, birthdays, anniversaries.

… Plan to succeed!

To Take Time to Talk

When I talk with families who are experiencing trauma, the issue of communication almost always comes up. Parents say of a child, "We can't get through to him"; a husband or wife will say, "We just don't talk anymore."

Times when communication is difficult occur in almost every family. When children hit the teenage years, it's not at all uncommon for them to go through a stage when you're lucky if you get a grunt as a verbal response. When Lloyd reached thirteen, he suddenly became incredibly uncommunicative. Dianne said to me one day, "I'm grieving the loss of the boy who used to follow me around telling me about his day." Normally with teenagers the problem passes, but in some relationships the lack of communication can be much more serious.

"A Creeping Separateness"

So many women I speak to complain of something that's hard to understand because they spend their lives surrounded by people. They often tell me they are lonely. One woman said, "I have an aching loneliness in my very being." But it's not just women who experience this. A husband said, "We don't seem to have much time for each other as a family. I can't remember the last time my wife and I had a real in-depth conversation."

None of us enters family life intending to be distant husbands, wives, mothers, or fathers, and in most families, lack of communication does not show itself quickly. But it becomes clear there's a problem when a teenage child who desperately needs to share her heart with her mother or father is unable to because there is no relationship there. And it becomes clear when a couple tell you they are divorcing and say, "It's not that we don't love each other – we do, in a kind of way. It's just that over the years we haven't seemed to have time for each other." One couple described this to me as "a creeping separateness".

When I have talked with couples who are going through a difficult time together, I have sometimes asked them, "If you could change anything about your relationship, what would it be?" Many men will say, "I wish my wife was more interested in sex." Of course, women mention sex as well, but it's far more common to hear them say, "I wish he was more *affectionate*."

We ask, "How could your husband show that to you?" And the reply will be something like this: "I want us to have time together. Time without the mobile phone going off. Time to talk and for him to give me the dignity of actually *listening*. I just want to know that I matter."

Rediscovering Communication

I've made some bad mistakes in this area. I've spent much of my life communicating with others but I remember well, in the early years of my family life, having little time for communication with those I loved most. I wrote about some of those mistakes in *The Sixty Minute Father*,[1] but thankfully I learned some lessons while my marriage was young and my children were small. I don't think Dianne and I would have made it had I not realized that our love was dying for lack of communication. At that time, I remember cancelling many commitments I had outside work and suddenly Dianne and I had evenings in which we had time for each other. This wasn't a quick fix – I remember during one particular winter that we spent night after night just talking.

The antidote to "a creeping separateness" and rediscovering communication with our partner and our children is not usually found in expensive holidays, or what some have called "quality time", but in quite a lot of "ordinary time" spent doing everyday things together – especially talking.

I think now of a couple I met some years ago. They had three children, led busy lives, and somehow they had grown apart. It seemed their marriage was at an end. Then they decided to give their relationship one last chance and to try something new.

They agreed that each Tuesday night they would spend the evening on their own together. Sometimes they went to the cinema, sometimes just for a walk, and very occasionally, a meal out. It's true they could afford babysitters, but they were not a wealthy couple by any means. It is simply that they made time with each other a priority and they *planned* it into their lives.

They had those Tuesday evenings together for at least twelve years and didn't tail them off until after their kids had left home. Did that evening every week save their marriage? Who knows? But I do know this: it became important to them. There was no point ringing them on a Tuesday night – their mobiles were turned off. Attempts to lure them to other things that occurred on what they came to call "our date night" were doomed to failure. It wasn't fancy, it wasn't expensive, but it did give to each of them the dignity of *time*.

They were wise; it's easy to make the mistake of pouring all our emotional energy into our children. Sociologist Christopher Lasch predicted thirty years ago "an emotional overloading of the parent–child bond".[2] He turned out to be a prophet. The problem with devoting everything to the children is that they grow older and, quite rightly, one day leave the parents behind – perhaps living far away. If we give ourselves totally to our children then when they're gone we may look at each other and ask, "Who are you?"

Of course it's not just communication with our partner that is vital, but communication with the whole family. This doesn't have to be complicated. It could be just chatting as we do ordinary things together – clearing out the garage, helping with homework, or cleaning out the rabbit hutch. Don't despise those ordinary conversations: research has shown that parental involvement has a huge affect on children's performance at school, and one of the most powerful elements of this is the time parents give to conversations about everyday events and activities. When those conversations did not take place – often because parents with young children didn't believe it mattered – it led not only to a lack of knowledge in the children but also to a lack of confidence.[3]

I remember acting on the advice of a friend who urged me to spend time with my children one-to-one. And whether it was football matches with Lloyd or drinking endless Coca-Colas with Katie, I discovered the sheer power of time together.

Spending time talking and especially taking time to *listen* is rarely easy, but it's an investment in the future. If we listen to our children when they are five, six, and seven as they're helping us wash the car – and making it worse – there's just a chance they'll listen to us when they are fifteen, sixteen, and seventeen.

Around the Table

It may be that we will rediscover communication around the meal table. In *The 7 Habits of Highly Effective Families* Stephen R. Covey talks of the power of mealtimes:

> We all have to eat. The way to the heart, the mind, the soul is often through the stomach. It takes careful thought and determination but it's possible to organize meaningful mealtimes – without television, without just gulping things down on the run. Family meals are important even if you only have one family meal each week.[4]

Jenny is a single parent mum. This is how she puts the importance of eating together as a family:

> I have three children aged between four and ten. I work full-time outside the home and life is hectic. Often the meals we eat during the week are on the run but on Friday evenings and Sunday lunchtimes

we eat "properly" as a family.

I've tried hard to make these meals special occasions. Each child has a task – helping with the cooking, laying the table, washing up – and although persuading the middle one to do anything at all is a battle every time, we usually get there eventually. On Fridays the meal could still be something ordinary like beans on toast, but we sit at a laid table and we talk. The telly's off.

I try not to have a go at the children during these meals – I want them to be enjoyable. And we always have a time when we can tell each other the best thing and the worst thing that's happened to us in the last week. Of course, getting a conversation going is sometimes like dragging teeth out – especially with the eldest one; but we've had some brilliant – and enlightening – times. Sometimes we play a game afterwards.

The other night I got home early on a Tuesday and they'd laid the table for a "proper" meal. One of them said, "I know it's not the right night, Mum, but can we do it anyway?" I thought, "Yes!"

I remember a woman telling me that when she was a child, there was an old wooden chair in her kitchen. When she was a baby, her mother nursed her in that chair. And it was holding the arm of that chair that she first stood and launched herself in an effort to master the art of walking. When she started school, she would run home and sit in that chair as her mother made the evening meal, and they would talk. As a teenager, she often sat there and poured out her heart to her parents.

She and her mother called it "the talking chair".

Lack of communication kills love and destroys families.

Both children and adults need a talking chair.

Action Points

If your children are small, cup their head in your hands and look into their eyes when they're trying to tell you something that is really important to them.

Ask your kids for their opinions on things – trivial and serious; it's part of their growing-up process. With a little one, "Which of these birthday cards do you think Sophie would like best?" or with a teenager, "I'm a bit worried about... What do you think I should do?"

Listening is hard! Try listening to somebody for two minutes without interrupting. One teenager said, "It was brilliant! My dad listened to me for *ages* without interrupting once. It feels great to be listened to."

Make sure you really listen, even if you think you know what the other person is going to say. It's a good idea to give small children some extra time to explain what they want to say.

Make the most of activities such as going for walks, doing jigsaws, washing up, or tidying a room where there's the chance to talk while you do it.

Wherever possible, try to eat a "proper" family meal together.

Plan regular one-to-one times with each member of your family – a game of pool with your son, a mother and daughter shopping trip, one parent taking a different child out each week for a Saturday breakfast.

Life Lesson 3:

To Discover the Power of Encouragement

In a recent radio interview I was asked the question, "If you could go back and live your family life over again, what is the one thing you would do differently?" I didn't have to think about my answer. I said, "I wish, in the early years, I hadn't tried to make people in my family be somebody they just couldn't be. If I had the chance again, I'd be more accepting of them. Instead of looking to see how they were matching my misplaced view of perfection, I'd take time to encourage them in the qualities and strengths they did have."

The Greatest Gift

One of the most important gifts that we can give to members of our family is acceptance. Unless people believe they are accepted it is hard for them to believe that they are *loved*.

I remember those times in my family life when I was not accepting; when I wanted to change everybody except

. I wanted Katie to be more sporty, like Lloyd. I wanted Lloyd to be more academic, like Katie. I wanted Dianne to be a little thinner, taller, more adventurous. But it's wearying to have somebody on your back who you just can't please because they want you to be somebody *else*. And the problem when you try to change somebody like that is that you miss the person they *are*.

I'm not exactly sure when it happened, but I changed. I began to appreciate the individual gifts and characteristics of my family – and to tell them that. Sure, Lloyd drove me crazy over his untidy bedroom and the fact that his geography teacher hadn't seen any homework since he was seven, but he had an incredibly caring heart for those who were down and out. And he could do what I only dreamed of – walk into a party and light it up. As I began not only to appreciate those qualities but to actually praise them, my relationship with him deepened. He began to believe that although any parent with an ounce of sense would have swapped his school reports for Katie's, I nevertheless valued the differences between them – and celebrated them.

It was the same with Dianne and Katie. I began, as an act of the will, to practise daily affirmation of the qualities they had, rather than carping criticism of the ones they didn't. Usually it's not possible to change somebody else, but you can change yourself. And the fascinating thing about change is that, especially in a close-knit group like a family, it is dynamic – often others then change as well.

Acceptance does not mean condoning bad behaviour or sarcastic speech. It's not giving up the hope of seeing positive change in another family member. It's rather the laying down of the personal mission to make another person – with all their incredible individuality – just like us.

I've shared some of my failures with you, so let me share a little success. My daughter Katie is married now. I promise you she is one of the least arrogant people you will meet, but she said to me recently, "You know, Dad, I feel pretty confident when I get into new situations, meet new people – just OK about myself. And I realized the other day that since I was small, you've said things to me like, 'You look good in that' or 'That meal you cooked was brilliant.' And I realized that the first man in my life accepted me, loved me, and made me feel I was special."

The Power of Encouragement

I'm sure we chanted lots of rhymes in the playground when I was a child, but the very silliest must surely be "Sticks and stones may break my bones, but words will never hurt me." If there were any lesson in life which I wish I could have discovered earlier, it would be to have understood the sheer power of the words we speak. Whenever you find families in which relationships are strong – whether they are wealthy or poor, stepfamilies, headed by two parents or a single parent, and whether they have 2.2 children or enough kids for a football team – you always find the same ingredient: the power of encouragement.

If I could rewind the clock, I would pay more compliments to Dianne instead of those silly carping criticisms I've sometimes been so fond of. When we went out, I would say more often, "You look great tonight" instead of helpfully pointing out, "Your hair looks funny."

I've just been to an awards ceremony for six young people aged between sixteen and twenty. Two had been excluded from school, one had just come out of prison, and all had in some way been disruptive to society. They had been on a course which taught them how to set life-goals, lift their self-belief, perform well in a job interview, and, wonder of wonders, how to give a talk in public.

What the course tutors didn't tell their students until the penultimate day of the course was that on the last morning they'd be asked to give a short presentation in front of fifty people.

I was privileged to be one of those fifty. As each young person took the floor, the tutors encouraged them. When the students faltered, they quickly came in with prompts to help them. And when each student finished their five-minute talk, the room erupted in applause, and each of the other students made a positive comment: "I noticed that Helen kept good eye contact"; "Amy was really funny and confident"; "Nathan made sure he had a really good ending"; "Gemma is always so warm towards people."

After the event finished, I stayed behind and talked with some of those who'd been on the course. I asked a girl of seventeen what had been special about it. She said, "I live in a dump. I've spent years hanging around street corners. All my life people have told me I'm a loser and that I always will be. But I've just given a talk to a room full of people and if I can do that, I can do anything. For the first time ever, I believe I can think about having a different kind of life."

These young people had been tutored for eight days by two people who didn't judge them for what they had done, who didn't pigeonhole them as losers, and who encouraged the slightest thing they did well. Eight days! Not eight years, months, or even weeks – eight days! Eight days experiencing the sheer power of encouragement.

Since we were married, Dianne and I have never experienced living in a traditional nuclear family. Over thirty years ago, a man who'd spent all his childhood in a care home and was practically homeless came to live with us for a short time. For some reason that none of us can quite remember, he never left.

He has some learning difficulties, and certainly when he first lived with us his self-esteem was very low, but from the day he came, Dianne began to encourage him whenever he did something well. I would hear her say, "Good job, Ron" or "You look nice today" or "Ron, you're a star!"

And slowly, month by month and year by year, Ron's belief in himself grew. He got a job and kept it and he's never been unemployed. He helped manage a football team and assists in a small charity that works with homeless people.

In the early days it was hard to find things to praise him for, but I watched Dianne search each day until she found something. Ron began to see his life in a different way: to see himself not as a failure but a success.

I knew that Dianne had done a great job when one day Ron came home from a cricket match. He is not a natural sportsperson so we were a little apprehensive in asking him how he had played. But we needn't have worried. I said, "How was the game, Ron?" A huge smile crossed his face and he said, "Great! I got two runs and *almost a catch.*"

If you want to bring out the very best in your children and your partner, then discover the power of encouragement. It should never be insincere, but it can be given for small things.

Affirmation can become an attitude. I sometimes see families that are being slowly destroyed by negative or sarcastic speech. I watch as husbands humiliate their wives in public with jokes over cooking or weight and hear partners trash in front of friends what the men in their lives have achieved. I gasp sometimes as parents tear holes in the tender self-esteems of young children, like the father who said to me as his thirteen-year-old daughter came into the room, "Look what the cat dragged in."

Sometimes the power of our parents' words is not diminished even when we are adults. One woman, who as a child rarely heard her mother praise her, recalled how on her wedding day her mother had remarked, "You look smart!" She said, "I didn't want to look smart. I wanted to look *beautiful.*"

But we cannot always give praise in our families. Sometimes we have to face somebody and say that what they've done is unacceptable and can't go on. Sometimes husbands and wives have to say hard things to each other, and certainly parents must be prepared to take knocks in the popularity stakes. But even when we have to say difficult things, it is easier and much more effective when it comes from lips that readily praise – where there is a history of affirmation. In fact, some research has suggested that to flourish as human beings

– to experience a sense of well-being – we need more positive comments than negative ones in our lives – to a factor of three to one.[5]

We can use encouragement even in extreme situations. Recently a mother came up to me at the end of one of the talks I give for the parents of teenagers and told me something of her story. Her son was sixteen and addicted to illegal drugs – in fact he'd spent time in a young offenders' institution. He'd been released the day before she came to the seminar.

She said, "Last evening I said to my son, 'Jack, please come in tonight before eleven o'clock; I worry when you're out late.'"

And then she said, "Rob, last night he came in on time, and it wasn't until I heard you tonight talking about encouraging our children that I realized I hadn't thanked him for that. When I go home tonight I'm going to tell him how much I appreciated his caring for me in that way."

This is a principle that is called "Catching your children doing something *right*". As mothers, fathers, step-parents – even as employers – we're used to catching people doing something wrong and criticizing them for it. But the faster and more effective way to improved behaviour is to catch them doing something *right* and encourage them in it. Many of us, even as adults, are crushed by the constant pointing out of where we go wrong. This is a great tragedy – when the ear never hears praise, the heart loses the will to try.

When you get the hang of catching people doing something right, you can often find the opportunity to encourage – even when it's not that easy.

The elderly grandmother went to watch her grandson at the school Sports Day. Tom didn't get into the final of the 100 metres or the 200 metres, and he was unplaced in the longer races as well. In fact the only event in which he looked remotely comfortable was the egg and spoon race, but even then he came last. As Tom and his grandmother walked away together the little boy's head was down until she put her arm around him and whispered, "You were the only one whose egg didn't fall off the spoon."

That young boy never did make it as a sportsman, but against the odds he did achieve great things in other areas of his life. I'm not surprised...

... It's hard to fail with a grandmother like that.

Action Points

Write a letter to your partner and each of your children – even those special members of your extended family – and tell them how much they mean to you.

Pop an encouraging note in your child's lunchbox or put one on your partner's pillow.

Buy or make a family organizer (the sort with a column for each person) and some fun stickers, and use it as a reward chart – for ALL the family – including Mum and Dad!

Catch your kids doing something right. If you're struggling for ideas, here are some to get you started:
- getting dressed by themselves
- being kind to animals
- telling a good joke
- watching out for lonely people
- remembering people's names
- being a loyal friend
- owning up to something
- helping with some tasks without being asked

It's worth doing for your husband or wife too!

Life Lesson 4:

To Decide *How* I Will Parent

Whenever I discuss parenting with people whose children are now grown up, I often perceive conflicting emotions at play. On the one hand there is sheer relief that they've at least managed to create the illusion that their kids have fled the nest (achieving the reality is normally a little more difficult). On the other hand there's often a sneaking desire for the chance of another shot at it.

This latter feeling is exceedingly fleeting, for it is tempered with the nagging belief that even if we could revisit those years and try to right all the mistakes we made last time, we would, in so doing, just make a whole lot of different ones. Nevertheless, at least for a while, nostalgia and guilt couple up and produce comments like, "Next time I'd be much stricter – I'd make him help much more around the house; I didn't do his wife any favours." Or perhaps, "Oh, I was just too strict. I see now that I might have crushed him sometimes. Next time I'd be more chilled."

The difficulty with looking back is that it's often futile. But it is certainly worth looking forward – to consider how we're going to parent while there's still time to effect change. The truth is that few of us choose a particular style of child rearing – we just do it, making it up as we go along. But that doesn't necessarily mean it's right.

Of course, the big question is, "When we consider the outcomes for the children involved, are some ways of parenting better than others?"

Trauma in the Maternity Ward

The young mother held her new baby in her arms, her husband hovering near, not completely sure of his ability to hold this precious bundle without dropping it.

"Now, before you leave the Maternity Unit there's just one more thing," the midwife said.

The mother looked distraught; she'd already pulled, pushed, panic-breathed, bitten her husband's hand, and come near to saying some words she hadn't used since she was in school. What more could there be?

The midwife smiled, "It won't take long. You just have to choose your parenting style, and then I can give you both a quick injection and you'll be on your way."

"Parenting style?" queried the father. "Can't we just work that out as we go along?"

"Certainly not," said the midwife. "That's how it used to be done, but nowadays we like to sort it out before you take baby home." And with that, she opened a drawer and took out four small boxes and a large syringe.

The husband nearly fainted. "Now calm down," said the midwife. "You'll hardly feel a thing. Which one would you like?"

The young mum looked near to tears. "Well, which would you recommend?" she said.

"Oh, I can't choose for you," said the midwife. "All I can tell you is what each one does and whether there are any dangerous side effects."

"What are the choices?" asked the father.

"Let me see," answered the midwife, looking at the instructions on one of the boxes. "This one gives you a life-time shot of overprotection towards your child."

"How does that work?" asked the mum.

"Well," said the midwife, "basically you wrap the child in cotton wool. You don't take them out in the pram if it's too cold, too hot, or if it's windy. You don't let them play with other children who have runny noses or if there's a rumour of nits in the family.

"As the child grows up, you arrange things so as to exclude the remotest possibility of danger. They're not allowed to engage in rough sports or play anywhere there could be a little dirt, and they never eat a single sweet. When they're teenagers, you take them to school in the car – even if it's just around the corner – and you always choose their friends for them, so avoiding the possibility of them mixing with kids who smoke, swear, or don't get their homework in on time."

The young couple looked at each other. "What do you think?" said the mum to her husband.

"Well, I suppose it would be alright," he said. "At least he'd always be safe." He turned to the midwife. "Are there any side effects with this one?"

The midwife turned the box over and read the notes on the back. "Side effects… hmmm… Oh, here we are:

" 'With this injection things tend to go reasonably well until the teenage years. By then some children have developed a growing resentment of the parents and in some cases are found screaming, "For goodness' sake, I'm sixteen. I don't want you meeting me from the party, carrying my warm overcoat."

" 'Even in cases where there are no problems in the teenage years, there is often total disaster later on when the child leaves home for university. Many fall immediately into a lifestyle of sex, drugs, and rock and roll, or alternatively get run over by a bus trying to cross the road on their own for the first time.' "

"Oh, dear," said the mum, "that's no good. Our job is to get him ready for life when we're not there to look after him."

The dad said, "I agree. We don't want that one."

"Well," said the midwife, picking up another box. "How about this: 'Anything Goes'?"

"How does that work?" asked the father.

The midwife read from the back of the box:

" 'After their injection, both parents will be filled with an overwhelming desire to please their child at any cost. Their mantra will be "If he wants it, he shall have it." In babyhood they will respond to every whimper immediately and retrieve the rattle every time the baby throws it out of the pram. In the toddler years, if their little one wants to urinate down the backs of neighbours' sofas, they won't discipline them or tell them to stop.

" 'As the child grows, they will gain the impression that they're the centre of the universe and that other people exist to make them happy. The parents will complain to the headteacher every time a teacher makes the child slightly unhappy – for example, shouting at them because homework isn't in on time.

" 'When the children are teenagers, the parents will develop an overwhelming desire to become their "best friend". This means they say yes to just about everything the child asks of them: requests for money; to come home late from parties; or even to stay out all night when they're fifteen. They will treat the child as a mature adult and even allow under-age smoking and drinking, and won't get too upset to find the occasional joint in the child's bedroom.'"

"I don't think I like the sound of that one," said the mother.

"I certainly don't," said the young dad. "I want us to be close, but I don't need to be his best friend – I'm his father for goodness' sake. My old man used to yell at me when I got in late, he'd threaten to ground me for a month if he caught me smoking, and he'd tell me to get out of bed that second when I told him I was too tired to get up for my Saturday job."

"Well, that's quite a speech, young man," said the midwife, quickly picking up another box. "You might prefer this one." She held the box up so they could see it – "Controlling Parents".

"It's a bit like the 'Overprotective' one but with a few bells and whistles on it." Her eyes scanned the instructions. "Now, let me see… ah… here we are:

"'After a single dose, the parents will want to control every aspect of their children's lives: the way they dress, their friends, hobbies, subject choices at school, boyfriends or girlfriends, career choice, kind of tricycle, cycle, car, or pogo stick. These parents want things done their way.'"

"What about side effects?" asked the dad.

"Let's have a look," said the midwife.

"'In some cases the child ends up hating the parents, can't wait to leave them, rebels at seventeen, joins a group of travellers, and the parents don't see them again until the children are in their mid-forties and living in a commune in Dorking.' "

The midwife could sense she was losing the battle and quickly snatched up another box. "This may be better," she said. "What about an injection of 'Impossibly High Standards'? With this one, nothing the child ever does is good enough; the parents criticize everything. The subliminal messages are: 'If a job's worth doing, it's worth doing perfectly' and 'Nobody remembers who came second.'

"Now, I know what you're going to ask," she continued, searching for the side effects section. "Right, let's see:

" 'In some cases the child will turn out totally screwed up and can't even enjoy their successes because they're scared they'll have to do even better next time. In later life they either give up totally or become so competitive they drive their loved ones crazy and bore their friends to death. They have little peace in their lives as adults and can't believe anybody could love them just as they are.' "

And with that, the midwife reached for another box, but the young man held up his hand:

"Look, I don't want to be rude, and I know that we've only just become parents and know almost nothing, but we do know we don't want to be like any of these.

"We don't want to be overprotective, but we do want to be cautious. We don't want to be permissive, but we want to say yes to our son when we think it's in his best interests. And if he gets the sack from his part-time job because he's always late, I'm going to tell him that that's how life is in the real world – not give him money to go out with his mates.

"My son's going to have plenty of best friends, but he'll

only have one mother and father, and we've got to be prepared to say the hard things – even if it means falling out with him once in a while.

"I don't want to be controlling, but I do want to be firm. And although our son will have to make lots of his own decisions as he gets older, I want him to know what I believe is best for him. But I realize he may not take my advice and I'll want him to know that I'll still be there for him in any case.

"And, finally, I don't want us to be critical. I want us to be encouraging, and if he comes second or last and he's tried his best, I want him to know that I'll be proud of him. I'm not stupid – of course I want him to fulfil his potential. But more than all of that, I want him to know that we'll love him anyway."

The midwife stood staring at the parenting injections in her hands and for a moment the young couple thought she was going to be cross, but instead she smiled and said, "The boxes were all empty, anyway. It's a little charade I go through with all the new mums and dads.

"You chose well – enjoy him."

The midwife seemed to offer quite a number of options in that situation, but in reality there are three main parenting styles:

Authoritarian

Parents who are authoritarian know how to put their foot down. Typical comments to the children are "Just do it!" or "Never mind 'why?' – it's because I said so" or "You will never do X or Y/wear clothes like that/listen to that kind of music while you are living under my roof."

If the family were the army, these parents would be the sergeant majors. They expect their orders to be obeyed instantly and don't encourage discussion.

Permissive

These parents are in some ways the opposite of the authoritarian type. They do not like either setting or enforcing boundaries, and they back away from confrontation. They are often warm and accepting of their children but rarely demand high standards in behaviour.

If the child of an authoritarian parent left his chocolate wrappers, shoes, and chewing gum on the floor in front of the television, he might expect to be yelled at and then grounded for a week. The child of permissive parents, however, would expect not only no reprimand at all, but also that his parents would probably clear it all up after him.

Authoritative

These parents believe that boundaries are important but are careful not to back themselves into a corner over things that don't matter. They are unlikely to hit the roof over minor issues, but on the other hand they will be very firm over things like curfews or homework before watching television. They take time to explain why the rules they set are important and are prepared to listen to an opposing view. Their children know they are accepted and loved, but equally know that Mum and Dad are not an easy touch. The children are encouraged to be independent.

With the authoritative parent, the child knows that

they are loved and affirmed. They often hear the parent say, "I love you" or "Well done." Even if the child is testing, the parent looks for ways they can affirm him. In short, the child is secure in the knowledge that although their parent has wishes for them – perhaps in terms of behaviour or achievement – they are loved unconditionally.

In the home there are as few rules as possible, but the child knows that the ones that are in place matter and that breaches of them have consequences. Many of the rules have been agreed between the family members.

Every parent will have their own views on discipline, but enforcing the rules is not just a matter of discipline; it is a matter of security. There is no faster way to breed insecurity in a child than for them to believe there are no boundaries – and that even if there are, nobody cares if they are crossed. I once saw a blind man walking along a long hospital corridor. He was tapping his white stick against the wall at the side of him. After a while he stopped tapping – he knew where the wall was. But after he'd gone almost the whole length of the corridor, I saw him reach out with his stick again and tap it against the wall a few times. He needed to test that it was still there – test where the boundaries were. Our children, too, will test the boundaries – push against them every now and then to test they are still there. They will actually feel more secure knowing they are in place. It is often exhausting and frustrating, but teaching our kids that boundaries matter is one of the major jobs of every parent.

One Mum Tries Something a Little Different...

Let's consider a typical family situation and observe the various parenting styles in operation.

Charlie is five years old and has been at his friend Tom's birthday party. His mum, Sarah, has turned up five minutes late to pick him up.

The second she gets into the friend's house, she can see that Charlie is in one of his bad moods. He yells, "Where have you been?" at her in front of the other mothers and refuses to thank his friend's mother for the party or even say goodbye to the other kids. He stalks out of the house towards the car. It takes her a good five minutes to get him into his car seat, and as she does he hits her across the head and knocks off her glasses.

Sarah is naturally a **permissive** mum. She will bribe, cajole, and sometimes practically beg Charlie to behave. If she deals with this in her normal way, the conversation will go something like this:

"Charlie, you really hurt me when you hit me over the head. Mummy is very sad and I never ever want you to do that again. And the next time you see Tom's mother, I want you to thank her for the party."

"No, I won't and I hate you." And with that Charlie will give the back of Sarah's seat a kick that will almost catapult her through the windscreen.

"Don't do that, Charlie..."

Sarah's friend Chloe is an **authoritarian** shouter, and on some occasions Sarah has been tempted to try her style. If she does, things might go something like this:

Sarah drags Charlie down the drive by his new school

49

jumper screaming, "Don't you EVER, EVER, EVER talk to me like that!" Charlie is then dumped pretty unceremoniously into the back of the car and lands somewhere near his seat.

When she gets home, it's likely that Sarah reverts to her permissive style. As she watches Charlie sulking, she begins to worry that she has damaged him emotionally forever. She starts to feel guilty and says, "Would you like a chocolate bar, Charlie? Come on, let's be friends again."

Charlie shouts, "No, I hate you." But later, as he's tucking into the chocolate, he smiles inside. He's in control again.

But in fact, neither of those scenarios actually pans out, because Charlie has the bad fortune of his mother having met another mum the day before who'd been on a parenting course. This mum had shared with Sarah a lesson she'd learned about **authoritative** parenting. Sarah decides to try it. She is filled with trepidation, because her friend said she'd have to be consistent and not back down once she started it...

On the drive home she simply ignores Charlie's rants, and eventually his tears. When she enters the house, she immediately begins tidying up as normal – seemingly uncaring about what has just occurred. Charlie looks a bit puzzled by this but at 5:30 he says, "Mummy, it's time to turn the television on for my programme." Without turning around Sarah says, "No, Charlie we're not having the TV on today." Charlie looks flabbergasted. "But we always have it on!"

"Yes, I know," Sarah replies. "But I didn't like the way you behaved earlier and I've decided not to put it on tonight."

That does it. Charlie goes into his normal routine – stamping, yelling, and eventually rolling on the floor crying. Sarah ignores all of this and simply goes on tidying the room.

Finally, when Charlie sees that his performance isn't working, he stops crying and says, "I'm sorry, Mummy. I won't ever do that again." Sarah immediately stops what she's doing, hugs him, and says, "I'm glad you said sorry, Charlie. That's OK. I love you."

Charlie says, "Can I have my programme on now, Mummy?"

Now here comes the brilliant bit. Sarah steels herself: "No, Charlie. When I said it wasn't going on tonight because of your bad behaviour earlier, I meant it."

Charlie immediately goes into the yelling, screaming, and rolling on the floor routine.

When Sarah finally puts an exhausted Charlie to bed she feels shattered herself, but as she watches him sleeping she thinks to herself, "For the first time since I became a mother, I feel a tiny bit in control."

So is the problem all sorted with Charlie? No, not yet. In fact, over the short haul his behaviour may well get worse. But the journey to better behaviour has begun, and in the future a small boy will, at least, have to consider a rule of life: actions have consequences – or in other words, "Don't diss your mother when there's something good on the telly."

Say What You Mean and Mean What You Say

Authoritative parents are not "picky" – in fact, as we've already said, they have as few rules as possible – but when their child crosses a line, that child knows there will be consequences. A fourteen-year-old girl may refuse to do the washing-up, but she will discover later that week that her pocket money is two pounds less than it was the week before. In short, with this type of parenting children know they are loved but also know that the rules matter. We can adopt this style even if it's not our natural one – but it helps if we begin early.

The problem is often that when our children are small we try to have boundaries (perhaps too many), but we never really expect them to be honoured. That means we end up making requests (or giving orders) to our children that we don't really believe will be met. And when they aren't met, we then start issuing threats that we have no intention of carrying out. The problem is that there are only so many "reallys" you can add – "The next time you do that you will really, really go to your room!" – without giving the game away that you don't mean to do anything at all. A basic principle in enforcing the boundaries is *"Say what you mean and mean what you say."* Consider this scenario:

Jessica is six years old and her mother says, "Jessica, it's five to six. Food's ready. Please put your toys away, wash your hands, and come to the table."

A few minutes later her mother says, "Jessica, I told you a moment ago – come and sit at the table."

About ten minutes later her mother says in a louder voice, "Jessica, I won't tell you again!"

But Jessica thinks to herself, "She will. She's only just got going. She'll probably tell me another ten times yet." And finally there's yelling and tears – probably from both Jessica *and* her mother.

The problem here is that the mum didn't mean what she said the first time. Let's rewind the tape and try it a little differently:

"Jessica, it's five to six. Food's ready. Please put your toys away, wash your hands, and come to the table."

(No action from Jessica.)

"Jessica, if you haven't put your toys away, washed your hands, and are sitting at this table by the time the long hand of that clock reaches the twelve, you are going straight to bed without anything to eat."

And suddenly Jessica is lying on her bed, clutching a digestive biscuit, and thinking, "What happened?"

What happened was that her mother said something and *meant it*.

The truth is that even with the very testing child the battles are easier to win when they are small, but you still have to be prepared to defend the boundaries – to show that they matter.

One mum, Sian, told me a wonderful story. She said that her toddler used to play her up whenever they went out, and she'd sometimes threaten to take him straight home. But she said she usually backed down because they had people to visit or the shopping to get or she'd already bought tickets for the cinema.

But one day, she had a brilliant idea. She took her son out when she didn't actually want or need to go out at all. And then she held her breath and hoped he would misbehave. When he did, she not only made the threat, but carried it out immediately. After two or three "false" trips he got the message, and his behaviour improved enormously.

Finding an effective style of parenting can revolutionize

our relationship with our children, but don't go into a flat spin and try to change overnight. And let me tell you a secret: when it comes to their own children, there are no "experts" – just people trying to get their own families through as best they can. So take what's useful from this book and discard what doesn't work for you. Nobody knows your child like you and nobody loves them like you. Styles of parenting like the ones we've considered above are useful – and I would urge you to consider them – but ultimately you must do what works for you in your family.

As we end this chapter, let me mention three warnings. First, don't think you can start down the permissive route and then suddenly swap to the authoritative one when the children are teenagers – it's much easier to let the reins out than pull them in. If you have toddlers, I would urge you to build up all the awe you can when they are small – you're going to need it later.

Second, if you have a partner, then stick together in enforcing the boundaries. There's not much use in a mum sending a six-year-old to bed early to teach him a lesson if his father goes straight upstairs when he gets in from work saying, "Don't worry, Son – she's always on at me as well."

And last, remember that whatever style of parenting you have, the most important thing is building a good *relationship* with your child – laughing, crying, playing, sharing together.

Rules without relationship lead to rebellion.

Action Points

Have a discussion with your partner – or if you're a single parent, with a friend – about parenting styles. Which is your natural style? Do you think any change would help?

Is it easy for your kids to play you off against each other? If you don't have a partner, do you feel that other people involved in your kids' lives – your parents, friends, or childminders – back you up?

Consider joining a parenting course – we can all learn something. (Many men tell us they were dragged there, but end up really enjoying it!)

Don't strive for perfection. Remember the letter the headteacher used to send home with the kids on the first day of school:

> *Dear Parent*
> *If you promise not to believe all that your child tells you goes on at school, I promise not to believe all that they tell me goes on at home.*

(Most parents were prepared to sign the deal in blood.)

Life Lesson 5:

To Love Enough to Let Go

I sometimes hear parents say, "I would die for my children." And, in many ways, the goal of parenting is to get them ready for that day: we have to prepare them to be able to live *without us.* Yet so strong is the desire in many parents to protect their children, they inadvertently make those children totally dependent on them. In doing so, they fail in one of the most fundamental tasks of being a mother or father.

Dianne and I have just received a text message. Our friends' baby has been born. That child is totally dependent on her parents. All 8 ¼ pounds of her can only survive if they exercise control over almost every part of her young life. But it's not just children we feel the need to protect. The desire to nurture, guard, and want the best for those we love is part of our role as family members.

How ironic that from this wonderful desire can often grow a compulsion that has the ability to destroy relationships. It is the need to control another person.

James is fifteen. When his mother first offered to give

him lifts to friends' parties he thought she was being kind. But then she insisted on dropping him off and collecting him from just about anything he was involved in – sports, social events, school, whatever.

It was the same when she bought him a mobile phone. He thought she was being generous. But now she wants him to ring her every two hours to tell her where he is and say that he's safe. She's just read that there's a phone available that as well as having many weird and wonderful gadgets, has a GPS device that will allow her to know to within 50 metres where he is twenty-four hours a day. She's said she's happy to buy it for him.

The other night James lied to his mother about where he was going and didn't phone to say he was OK. When he got home, she'd rung every one of his friends and discovered he'd deceived her. She grounded him for a week.

Ben and Emma have been married for two years, and at least once a week Ben's mother Esther has stopped in at their home to deliver "one of Ben's favourite meals". She says it is "to give Emma a night off from cooking after a long day at work".

What Esther has never seen is the sight of each of those meals going into the waste bin untouched, so at least she's not upset. But that's the easy part. The really tricky bit is whether Ben will have the courage to tell his mother that actually he's married now and although her actions seem kind, they're making it harder for Emma and him to live their own lives.

Driven by Fear

There are many reasons why family members want to control others. Perhaps the most understandable is fear.

This emotion can sometimes be seen in the relationship between a husband and a wife.

Neil's marriage to Clare is near to breakup. In the counsellor's office she tells of years of enduring her husband's mistrust. She says, "He's consumed by the belief that I'm going to have an affair. He hasn't got a single reason to suspect that, but he won't even let me have a conversation with another man unless he's around. I find him going through my handbag, and he wants to know where I am every minute of the day."

The counsellor turns to the husband. "Is that how you see it?"

Neil nods. "She's right. I just can't seem to help it. When my mother hit forty, she left us to go off with a colleague from her office. Clare is thirty-nine."

But so often it's in the parent–child relationship that we see fear really come into its own. Let's face it, that's not hard for parents today – after all, there are so many things of which to be afraid. But it becomes a problem when we cross a boundary from a proper and healthy concern about our children into a dark and destructive place in which we're constantly filled with soul-gnawing anxiety for those we love. And it has no end: as soon as one situation is resolved, another rears its head.

It's easy to understand how this can happen to parents with children who are especially challenging, but the tragedy is that when this emotion runs unchecked, kids who are displaying no more than normal disobedience or some minor rebellion can seem, in their parents' eyes, to be about to ruin their lives forever. This fear then drives those parents to revert to what they did when their children were babies – keep them from harm by controlling every part of their lives. As adults, some of these children can never forget the suspicion, sense of disappointment, and failure that this engendered in their parents towards them.

"Catch, Challenge, Change"

When my kids were small they used to love the "Mr Men" series, and I must admit I identified most closely with Mr Worry. He would worry about everything and anything. And if there was ever a day when he was not concerned about anything at all, he would convince himself he'd missed something and that would make him really worried. It's a danger that we live like him as parents. Mark Twain said: "Most of my tragedies have never happened to me." Twain is right, and unless we remember what he said, we'll so exhaust ourselves worrying about what *might* happen that we'll have few emotional reserves to deal with the challenging situations that actually do come along. So often, this is a battle of the mind.

I used to find my fears multiplied when my thoughts ran away with me. One of the kids would be ten minutes late coming home, and pretty soon I was hearing ambulance sirens. Or perhaps I'd find a cigarette butt under Lloyd's bed, and within moments I was imagining him buying drugs on the street and trying to get Katie in on the deal.

And then a psychologist friend told me about "Catch, Challenge, Change" – a device that helps you stop runaway fears. It's simply that when those first negative thoughts come into your mind you catch them – stop them running away; then challenge them – "No, this is not reality"; and finally replace them with something more reasonable – "This is a cigarette butt, not heroin. I'll need to talk to him, but it's a phase many of us have gone through." "Catch, Challenge, Change" has helped me deal with the runaway thoughts that breed fear and drive me to the need to control.

The need to control may have many roots, not least the worry about what other people are thinking of our children's behaviour – and therefore of our parenting. We'd be wise to lay down this particular worry as soon as possible – life's hard enough without trying to win a parenting Oscar.

Time to Back Off a Little

In addition to fear, perhaps the most common reason given for the desire, or even the need, to control is, "I just want the best for them." Karen and Jeff have two children. Meg, the eldest, is compliant, works hard at school, and is a dream to have around the house. Harry, two years younger, is consumed by football, hates anything that smells of reading, writing, or exams, and tests his parents to the extreme almost every minute of his young life.

With Harry approaching his exams, Karen has worked additional hours so they can afford to send him to a tutor for five of his subjects. But she often gets home from work to discover he hasn't gone to the extra lessons. The other day she found all the study guides she'd bought him under his bed, still in their cellophane wrappers.

The other night Harry told them he had to get his English coursework in by the next day or it would be too late. Jeff and Karen stayed up half the night writing two essays while Harry lounged on the sofa watching television and calling out occasionally with helpful hints as to the general direction they might want to take. They are exhausted.

And the trouble with Harry isn't just over his schoolwork. Karen has to wake him up for his football matches, find the football boots he's lost, and pay his mobile phone bill because he's got no money since he got fired from his Saturday job. She feels like the man in the circus who is balancing spinning plates and that Harry is in the audience throwing new ones to her every day.

The difficulty with controlling others is that although our basic motivation is often good, the results are almost always negative. Somebody once said, "Good judgment is based on experience and experience is based on bad judgment." The problem when we take so much control of our children's lives that we try to make everything turn out right for them is that we rob them of the learning process that comes with a little pain.

This is hard for parents to grasp because we spend our lives protecting our children and keeping them from being hurt. We see them across the road, we warn them not to talk to strangers, we watch what they eat. But if children go through their childhood being totally cosseted, they enter the adult world stunted. The other day I listened to a university student talk to a television reporter about her mother. She said, "She wouldn't let me travel anywhere on my own. She drove me to everything. And after she read about a girl who died on an outward bound course, she refused to even think about my going on a school trip. The only problem is I'm eighteen now, living away from home, and I don't even know how to catch a bus."

Karen and Jeff, the parents we talked of above, will one day discover that there's something worse than Harry failing an examination, missing a football match, or not saving enough to pay his mobile phone bill. It will be the first time he experiences the real consequences of those things as an adult – when, perhaps, they're not around to help him. By then, however, it won't be his homework – it'll be a report for his boss. And it won't be a football match he has to get up for – it'll be his job. And it won't be his mobile phone bill – it'll be his mortgage.

Of course, sometimes the desire to "put everything right" is not as altruistic as we imagine. It may be that we've grown to like, even *need*, being needed. But whatever the reason, the bag of total responsibility we carry on our backs is too heavy to bear, and we become more effective husbands, wives, or parents when we set it down.

But perhaps the greatest danger with a controlling personality is that it makes it hard for relationships to flourish. We've all had friends who want to control us. They comment on the way we dress and the kind of car we drive. They like to organize our lives and have an answer for every trauma we experience. The trouble is that while such relationships sometimes work when we feel dependent on our friends, sooner or later we become exhausted by their need to control us. When we later tell other friends why we no longer see them we say, "She suffocated me" or "I felt I couldn't be myself around him."

It can happen to our children. They come to see the family home not as a nest from which they need to fly, but as a prison from which they must escape.

Some of us naturally have the kinds of personalities that make us feel responsible. We feel responsible for *everything*. A friend is made redundant and we think, "How can I get her a job?" We watch a television report of a disaster on the other side of the world and feel frustrated we're not there to help. It rains on the day of our friend's wedding and we think, "I wish I could sort this for them." Whether it's the job, the earthquake, or the weather, we not only feel we want to help but that we should be able to do *something*.

Of course, in some ways these desires are good. But with this kind of personality, relationships in our family life can be very hard – especially in situations where our need to put things right meets the spectre of fear for those we love.

We get to a stage where we feel responsible for the mistakes our husband, wife, or children make. This leads us to try to put all those mistakes right, which, as we've seen, is neither possible nor often even desirable. With our older children and partner we have to realize that they'll make their own choices – and sometimes those may be bad ones.

Of course we want to influence those we love, give our advice and offer our opinions, but we should realize that our role is limited. We can do something to help, but not *everything*. Some years ago in Cardiff Crown Court, a man of eighty-two was sentenced to seventeen years' imprisonment. He protested to the judge, "Your honour, I'm over eighty. I'll never make it." Apparently the judge looked at the prisoner over his spectacles and said, "Do what you can."

Anyway, there's a very good reason to try to get this particular issue sorted. One old hand at parenting put it well: "The problem with trying to control your kids is: if you fail, you'll never see them again; if you succeed, you'll never get rid of them."

Do what you can.

Action Points

Consider whether there are any areas of your children's lives where you are overprotecting them from the consequences of their actions. What could you do to help them learn from these situations?

Plan some "letting go" actions, depending on the age of your children:

- Teach them their address and phone number – but explain when and where not to share them.
- Talk through possible emergency scenarios with them – what would they do?
- Plan a journey on public transport.
- Give them three pots for their pocket money – "spend, save, and give away" – to teach them budgeting.
- Let them earn some money and then buy Christmas and birthday presents for the family with the earnings.
- Allow them to cook dinner – older children can choose the menu and buy the ingredients.

In the UK, do the "Quidz In" course for parents to help you raise financially confident kids. Visit www.quidzin. org.uk for details.

Link your children's pocket money to jobs that are actually done well – if they think you're being unreasonable, wait until they get a boss!

Life Lesson 6:

To Handle Conflict Effectively

Families fight. They fight about money and which computer games belong to whom. They fight about cleaning rotas and which channel the television should be on, about in-laws, cleaning out the guinea pigs, and which relatives should be visited at Christmas. They fight about homework, about rudeness and curfews... Families fight.

And it starts pretty young, even with toddlers and toys...

Property Law According to a Toddler

If I like it, it's mine.
If it's in my hand, it's mine.
If I can take it from you, it's mine.
If I had it a little while ago, it's mine.
If it's mine, it must never appear to be yours in any way.
If I'm doing or building something, all the pieces are mine.

If it looks just like mine, it's mine.

If I saw it first, it's mine.

If you are playing with something and you put it down, it automatically becomes mine.

If it's broken, it's yours.

When Home is a Battleground

The truth about most family conflict is that it is both inevitable and passing. You hear siblings say when they are adults, "We get along fine now, but when we were kids we fought like cat and dog" or "My mother and I used to row about everything, but now we're more like best friends."

But while it's true that most family conflict is both normal and temporary, it's also true that some families seem to exist in a perpetual state of conflict. These homes are constantly filled with raised voices, frayed nerves, and bitter comments. Such families are not a haven from a stress-filled world, but a battleground in the middle of it.

Conflict such as this usually comes with a high price tag. Children are often much more resilient than we may think, but when they are in a family in which conflict is serious and doesn't get resolved, they can begin to see it as a threat to themselves and become anxious. One fourteen-year-old boy put it like this: "I think all kids should have the right to live in a happy place where they feel safe and loved. I haven't felt like that in some time, but I know my parents don't mean it. It's just that they argue and take it out on me."[6]

Sometimes children will blame themselves for family arguments and become withdrawn or depressed. And sometimes the children of such homes never learn how to deal with conflict and replicate the problem when they start their own families.

But more important than how much conflict we have in our family is how we resolve it. If we won't listen to our children without interrupting, then we'd better not expect them to listen to us. If we use bad language and personal insults in conflict situations, then we should get ready to hear that from them. And if we won't compromise with our kids – just watch them learn to dig their heels in. The problem here is not that our children aren't listening to us, but that they *are*.

Something in the Bank...

Strong families don't avoid conflict; they develop effective strategies to deal with it. But before we look at some strategies, let's first consider the foundation stone of dealing with conflict effectively: strong relationships.

Stephen R. Covey talks about making "emotional deposits" in each other's lives.[7] These are positive experiences that others have of us. That's why I began this book with the issue of "time" – because building up those deposits takes lots of it. And often it's by doing seemingly insignificant things: reading stories, playing games, watching our son in endless football matches, listening and trying to understand as our partner shares a worry about their work life, being there in practical ways when our husband or wife is ill, or helping solve a problem that may not seem large to us, but matters to our child.

"Emotional deposits" help another family member to believe that we love them, want the best for them, and are on their side. The effect of this is that when conflict does come they can listen to our point of view more easily, not be so deeply hurt by some of our comments, and, if necessary, forgive us faster. Sometimes we have to say hard things to each other, but they are easier to take if they come from somebody who has demonstrated a history of commitment to us. The book of Proverbs says, "Faithful are the wounds of a friend."

I remember having to draw on those emotional bank deposits with Lloyd one day when he was in his mid-teens. We were going through a tough time in our relationship and were having a row because I didn't want him to go out and he was determined to. I stood in the doorway of his bedroom blocking his way. He then squared up to me, and for a moment it looked as though we could soon be rolling around on the floor fighting each other.

And then I moved away from the door and sat in a chair in the far corner of the room and said, "I don't deserve this from you, Son." His way was now clear to go. And in my heart was the question, "Do we have enough history of good times together to see us through this?" He hesitated for a moment, then sat on his bed and we talked.

Those years with Lloyd as a teenager were turbulent at times. But I am scared to even consider what they might have been like if we'd not had years behind us of doing things together – laughing, playing, talking – to help get us through: in other words, putting a little credit in that emotional bank.

Of course, this can be particularly difficult for a step-parent who is suddenly in a relationship with a thirteen-year-old stepchild – perhaps with few or no deposits in the bank at all. It is often wise to concentrate on building those emotional deposits with care and patience, rather than suddenly imposing our own parenting style.

Some Dos and Don'ts

Even a good relationship on its own is not enough. We need some strategies to help us deal with conflict. Here are some dos and don'ts.

1. Don't attack somebody's person. Your child will get over your saying, "Come on, if you work a bit harder you can get this 'C' up to a 'B' ", but you can scar them for life by saying, "If you don't pull your socks up, you're going to be a loser for the rest of your life."

   Similarly, your partner may be able to handle a row about her missing your daughter's dental appointment, but expect long-term trouble if you start using phrases like, "You're such a lousy wife and mother."

2. Don't compare people: "I wish you were more like Carol's husband." (It's not impossible that Carol is daydreaming about your man.) And parents who compare siblings can drive wedges between them which some of those kids never recover from – even in adulthood.

3. Don't exaggerate: "You never..." "You always..." "You are the worst..."

4. Don't trivialize. Sometimes conflict arises because somebody believes the other family members don't understand what they're going through.

Dealing with this isn't easy because often it's our role as a parent or partner to help them put what they're going through in perspective. However, this only ever works if the other person knows you are at least trying to understand them. My mother was great, but I never appreciated the way she used to meet every one of my broken hearts with the words, "Never mind. There's plenty more fish in the sea."

So whether it's the loss of a job, a fourteen-year-old breaking up with a girlfriend, or a dead goldfish, give them the message: "If this matters to you – it matters to me."

5. Don't avoid discussion. Give the other person a chance to speak without interrupting – and listen. But when it's your chance to talk, remember that it can be very effective to not just complain about people's behaviour – "You always leave your shoes/chocolate wrappers/ dirty dishes on the floor in front of the TV" – but to let them know how that behaviour makes you feel – "When you leave your shoes/ chocolate wrappers/dirty dishes on the floor in front of the TV for me to clear up, I feel you just take me for granted."

6. Do stick to the issue – don't dig up dirt from the past. "I'll never forget when you…" Every marriage has two or three old bazookas that the couple bring out in time of conflict. Lay them down – if only to find new ones.

7. Do try to find creative solutions that take differences of perspective into account. One of the greatest challenges in dealing with conflict is that families are made up of people who often have quite different personalities. And that means they deal with relationships differently. When we might think another family member is being evasive, they think they're being diplomatic; and when they think they're being objective, we think they're being uncaring. Keep your requests for a change in behaviour reasonable – don't expect a personality transplant.

8. Do try to cut each other a little slack at times of particular stress – perhaps when one family member is facing examinations, loss of a job, a relationship breakup, or a falling out with a best friend.

9. Do remember that the silliest line in any film is found in the blockbuster Love Story: "Love means never having to say you're sorry." In fact the opposite is true: "Love means always having to say you're sorry."

10. Do focus on developing trust. Insist on honesty (but not blame). Be prepared to forgive and apologize. Remember the old Chinese proverb: "The man or woman who will not forgive must dig two graves."

Finally, one more strategy that can head off conflict at

the pass is to ask this question: "Why is this such a big deal to me?" I used to sound my horn at people who "cut me up" when I was driving. I don't do that now for several reasons. First, they hear your horn. And second, when they've heard it, they sometimes get out of their car and try to get into yours. And as they are beating you about the head you are thinking, "Why was that such a big deal to me?" In other words, "Was the potential conflict worth it?"

You Can't Fight Them All

Some of us have personalities that mean we just can't help ourselves pointing out something that bothers us. The problem with that in family life is that we're always picking on something – which means that conflict is never far away.

If we choose to point out and do battle over every possible issue with our children – whether it's putting the toys away, tidying the bedroom, homework, tucking their shirts in, rudeness, smoking, curfews, loudness of music, hairstyles – then there will be very few days when there's no conflict in our home. Or perhaps, even worse, there will be days when all is quiet but a child is building up bitterness inside because "my mother is always nagging me".

Of course, it's vital that we fight some battles – but if we choose to fight them all, then our family will believe that "Dad is always on our backs!" and, worse, they'll never know when something *really* matters to us – the nagging over the shirt hanging out will merge with the nagging about the smoking.

Asking "Why is this such a big deal to me?" is not

only useful in our relationship with our children, but with our husband or wife. Somebody said, "Women marry men with the foolish notion that they'll be able to change them; and men marry women with the silly idea that they'll be the same forever." We can have very high expectations, and when those aren't fulfilled we can become critical or carping. But every relationship is a compromise. We can't have it all. Of course sometimes we'll need to tell someone in the family that they are behaving badly – whether it's our children or our partner. But even if that's necessary, it's normally best to do it when our emotions aren't running high. If you feel you're about to explode, try to hold your tongue for a moment and ask yourself three questions:

- Is this really important to me?

- When I look at the facts, is my anger justified?

- How can I contribute to the solution?

In other words, before you "sound your horn" in your family, think twice – they may hear it.

Action Points

Have a regular "Family MOT (tune-up)" – perhaps over a visit to the pizza parlour. Here are some questions that will help you decide whether your car's in good shape or could do with a bit of repair work!

- **Mechanical soundness:** What things do we enjoy doing as a family? How could we do more of them?
- **Rattles and squeaks:** What frustrations do we have in our relationships as a family? How could we tackle them?
- **Mileage:** What would we like to achieve as a family in the coming year?
- **Exterior bodywork:** How could we help others outside our family?

Ask yourself at least once a day, "Why is this such a big deal to me?"

Remember the conflict checklist:
- Is this really important to me?
- When I look at the facts, is my anger justified?
- How can I contribute to the solution?

It won't always be possible, but a really good solution is one that will work for everyone.

Life Lesson 7:

To Experience the Magic of Traditions

My friend had died, and I visited his wife and grown-up children to discuss what they wanted me to say at his funeral. I said, "Tell me some of your most precious memories." Their eyes filled with tears and then his daughter, a woman in her mid-twenties, spoke up. "On Saturday nights Dad always did the cooking. He wore a special apron and we'd call him Edna – which was the name of our dinner lady in school."

His son said, "At about five o'clock on Saturday afternoons we'd begin to shout, 'What's on the menu, Edna?' and he'd always reply in a silly French accent, 'Edna never tells!'"

"We weren't allowed in the kitchen on those nights – not even Mum – and finally he'd emerge shouting, 'Edna has created another masterpiece.'"

The daughter broke in, "Dad wasn't a great cook – he wasn't even a good cook. Some evenings it would go horribly wrong and we'd hear the car start outside.

We knew then that 'Edna' would be 'creating' fish and chips that night. But whatever Dad made, we'd eat it together while watching a film. He hardly missed a Saturday."

"We Always..."

My friend's family could have spoken of many memories of their father – perhaps holidays they'd had or special gifts he'd given them – but when I asked them to recall one of their most *precious* memories, their minds went to a family tradition.

I can't say I was surprised. Over the years, I've had the opportunity of talking with thousands of individuals about their childhood, and time and again those who spoke of strong families also spoke of traditions. Whether these families were rich or poor, lived in the country or the inner city, were headed by a mother and father or a single parent, their response was often the same. When I asked them to tell me what made the memories of their family life sweet, sooner or later they'd start a sentence with, "We always..."

The traditions people have shared with me have been many and varied. They are often to do with special days of the year. One family said they always light candles on Christmas Eve and watch *It's a Wonderful Life*. Another family always go for a walk in a busy park on Boxing Day, and as people come towards them they try to guess what presents they are wearing! One family sings "Auld Lang Syne" holding hands together in the street outside their home on New Year's Eve and then has a curry afterwards, sharing hopes and dreams for the year ahead around the table.

Of course sometimes those telling me their stories realized that the memories they were sharing were simple ones – even a little embarrassing. But once they got the confidence to talk to me, then no matter how old they were, the traditions came tumbling out. One very sophisticated lawyer told me she remembered having the following conversation with her father every evening when she was small:

"Daddy, can I sit on your lap?"

"No. Only little girls with brown eyes can sit on my lap."

"I've got brown eyes!"

"Well, only little girls with brown eyes and black hair can sit on my lap."

"Daddy, I've got brown eyes and black hair!"

"Well, only little girls with brown eyes, black hair, and pink shoes can sit on my lap…"

… And finally a small child with brown eyes, black hair, pink shoes, and some nights a dozen other attributes, would climb onto her father's knee. And when she was old, she still remembered it.

"A Sense of Connectedness"

The family acts as a bulwark to the storms of life outside. It should be a place of training, security, and safety, but it also has another vital function. It gives us a sense of belonging – of roots; it helps us know our place in the world – perhaps, even, the universe.

Traditions are a part of this, and whether they belong to the national culture – like setting off fireworks on 5 November in the UK, cooking a turkey on Thanksgiving Day in the USA – or simply having fish and chips on a

Saturday night, they create what someone once called "a sense of connectedness".

Having this "sense of connectedness" is harder today. We're not only more isolated from neighbours and extended family outside the home, but from each other *inside it*. It's quite likely that on any given evening five members of a family will be scattered throughout the house playing different computer games, watching different television programmes, or listening to different music. The older our children, the harder it is to do anything about this, but that needn't stop us trying. Many families have found that a good place to begin to re-establish a sense of connectedness is around the table. Marianne Jennings is professor of legal and ethical studies at Arizona State University. She speaks of the power of that simple piece of furniture in the tradition of her childhood:

> I cut my wedding dress on the same table where I memorized my spellings. It was in that same place that I ate Archway Cookies after school. And it was there that I prepared for my exams. My future husband was grilled mercilessly in that same spot. Much of what I have learned in life is inextricably intertwined with that kitchen table. This four by six scratched and worn piece of furniture was a small physical part of my home, and yet as I look back on what we did there, I realize it was a key to the life I now have.[8]

Don't relegate the humble table to some past "golden age of the family" – there never was such a time. The fact is that whether it's eating together, working together, or playing together, the table can be a focal point in our family life.

Recently, I spoke to a colleague who'd been running a parenting course, in which they had talked about the importance of family mealtimes. At the end of the session, Hannah, a single parent, came up to the course leader and said, "We don't have a table in our home and I can't afford one." They came up with the idea of laying a blanket on the floor and sitting around it. Hannah went home saying she'd try it. But at the start of the following week's session she said, "After I left last week I passed a second-hand furniture shop on the way home and in the window was a table and four chairs. I put a small deposit on it and the owner is going to keep it for me as long as I pay a little off the balance each week."

And that's exactly what she did until one day she walked into the class and announced, "Today my table and chairs are being delivered! Yes!" What she didn't know was that the other parents in the group had been getting ready for this moment, and when she finally sat at the table with her family it was decorated with flowers, candles, and the biggest cake they'd ever seen.

When I wrote the first book in the "Sixty Minute" series, *The Sixty Minute Father*, I spoke of a tradition that used to take place in our family when our children were young. Once a week they would drag their mattresses across the landing and sleep on our bedroom floor. We called it a "Family Night".

And once a month we would have a "Super Family Night". This was a little more complicated and involved us all dragging our mattresses downstairs and sleeping on the living room floor. Now there's no good reason why four people with perfectly good beds upstairs should want to do that – except that it's fun. We'd light the fire, eat chocolate, and tell stories in the darkness.

That little book sold in over a dozen languages, and it seems that the idea of "Family Nights" caught on. I began getting letters from across the globe telling me of parents and kids dragging their beds downstairs.

But the feedback wasn't all positive. Once, when I was giving a seminar in Canada, a man approached me as I entered the auditorium. He looked cross. He said, "You're Rob Parsons, aren't you?"

I was tempted to say, "No, I'm the caretaker", but I admitted it.

He said, "I have four kids and we tried the whole 'Super Family Night' thing. You know – beds downstairs, stories in the dark, and eating chocolate."

I nodded nervously. He went on, "Three of my kids were sick all over their mattresses, and the fourth threw up in my wife's car the next day." Then a huge smile crossed his face and I realized he wasn't cross at all. "It was worth it, though," he said. "Thanks for the memory."

As he walked back to his seat I thought about what he'd said: how the silliness, the hassle – even scraping the sick from the back seat of the Volvo – was worth it. Don't despise traditions. Whether they are simple or profound, in our family or in our nation, traditions say to us, "You belong here – these are your roots."

Traditions are not always so easy. For example, they can be challenging for a new stepfamily with different ways of doing things. One mother told me how she'd tackled bringing together quite different Christmas traditions in her blended family:

> I brought my three children with me to live with my new husband and his two sons. As we discussed preparations for our first Christmas together, we realized we had different traditions. So we decided to create some new ones. Stepdad and my youngest child went to choose the Christmas tree together – which has happened every year since then. But it wasn't all so easy. His children were used to having stockings at the end of their beds on Christmas morning which they could open as soon as they awoke. My children had to wait and always had everything downstairs. So we added these traditions together so they all had stockings by their beds with smaller presents in and then had larger presents in the lounge which we opened together. Everyone was pleased!

Of course it's not just children for whom traditions are important. They can help cement a marriage – whether it's having a weekend lie-in listening to Steve Wright's *Sunday Love Songs* on the radio ("Chance would be a fine thing!" say the couple with toddlers), getting away over an anniversary weekend, using silly phrases that mean a lot to the couple but nothing to anybody else, candles on a Saturday night, swapping resolutions on New Year's Eve, or simply never going to sleep without a kiss.

Traditions are powerful. If you don't believe me then talk to any adult you know who had a happy family life.

Ask them to tell you what made it special and pretty soon they'll say, "We always…"

Action Points

Start a memory box with your partner and each of your kids. Fill it with little treasures and mementoes. Every so often, get it out and look through it together.

Keep a family quote book – funny, embarrassing, profound.

Use that table! Encourage your family to find some of its entertainment *together*. It might take a while to get the kids through the pain barrier, but rediscover board games.

On New Year's Eve, have a family meal together and challenge each other to name ten highlights of the year just gone.

Sleep out in the garden under the stars once a year and have a midnight feast.

Create a bedtime ritual – maybe a special prayer, a quiet song, or a story read by Mum or Dad.

Visit www.careforthefamily.org.uk/memorable-moments to read some great ideas from other families.

Life Lesson 8:

To Learn to Love in January

We all want to give our families the best. But what is that? Somebody once said that the greatest gift parents can give their children is to love each other. In my work supporting all kinds of families, I've seen too much pain on a daily basis to believe that there are easy answers to the problem of family breakup. Nevertheless, the idea that children escape the breakup of their parents' marriage unscathed is usually both wrong and naïve.

"For the Sake of the Kids"

People say, "Children are better out of a home in which there is conflict", and of course this is sometimes the case. But the truth is that the conflict doesn't disappear the moment a family breaks up. And, anyway, even when there has been conflict, the children often still love both parents – and want both parents. Of course, children can come through the breakdown of their parents' relationship, but it will help us as parents to support and guide children through this time if we can understand something of what many of them feel.

One father whose marriage had broken up wrote to me and said this:

> It dawned on me after a while what was happening with my children and I'm sure with lots of kids who go through this. We may fall out of love with each other, but our children do not fall out of love with us. They become expert in concealing rather than sharing their emotions. When they are with Daddy, they learn not to talk about Mummy. They are careful about sharing holiday photographs in case one parent sees them having a good time with another. They run parallel lives. At Christmas the kids don't tell their parent what gift they got from the other – and which separated parent doesn't feel a sense of fear that if their gift is inferior to the other parent's, somehow the child will think that parent loves them more?

Over the years I have listened to the stories of many people who have experienced family breakup, but one small boy sticks out in my mind. He was ten years old and his father had just left his mother. Sitting on a step outside his house, he looked up, and said, "My father doesn't love my mother anymore and he has left us now – what does a kid do?"

But it's not just young children who feel this. Laura Telfer, a relationship counsellor with the UK charity Relate for eighteen years, says that splitting up when the children are older can seem like an attractive option: "There is definitely a susceptible time when the children leave home when all possibilities seem open. But it does not make the unexpected desertion any easier. What can be an exciting venture for one partner is invariably a painful grieving episode for other family members. Children watch appalled as their family, that secure and safe place that survived all their childhoods, is swiftly dismantled."[9]

But if it's true that there are no easy answers when a couple's relationship breaks down, then it's also true that many people begin their married lives together with not even the gentlest warning of something that will have to be faced if their relationship is to last.

January Love

It is my friend's daughter's wedding day and I've been asked to say a few words at the service. In many ways this is a perfect day: the bride looks wonderful; her husband-to-be is like a handsome prince; the sun is streaming through the stained glass windows of the old church. As I sit waiting for my part in the service, I watch the young couple. I can see they have eyes and ears only for each other. I sigh inwardly and remind myself that in such circumstances I would be wise not to take myself too seriously. I tell myself that, for them, listening to this old guy for a few minutes is part of the deal – and, hopefully, a part that will soon be over.

I consider what I intend to say and debate whether or not I dare speak of the issue that's on my mind. As I am still thinking, I hear my name being called and I rise from my seat to walk to the front of the little church. Even as I walk, I am wondering if I dare mention it and then quite suddenly I decide.

"I want to talk to you today about January love," I say.

"I often go to write my books in a small cottage in West Wales. One August afternoon, I took a break and was walking on the beach. It was a wonderful day. The sun shone out of a cloudless sky. Behind me, part-framing the bay, were patchwork hills, and in front of me the sea shimmered in the summer heat. It felt good to be alive. I walked along the beach then made my way back to the cottage. As I reached the road, I saw an old fisherman sitting on a bench. 'It's glorious, isn't it?' I said. I don't know if he was having a bad day or just tired of tourists, but he said, 'You should see it in January.'

"The next day, I walked on the beach again. It looked as lovely as it had twenty-four hours before, but this time I imagined the hills, the bay, and the sea whisper to me, 'Will you love us in January?'"

I could see that many of the wedding guests in the old church were listening to me intently. Those with older heads and hearts that had experienced some pain knew what was I was about to say, but the young couple looked at me quizzically. "Today, for you, this is summer," I said. "You both look wonderful, the setting is perfect – who could not love on such a day? But will you be able to love in January?"

I went on to tell them that I believed there is no relationship that does not, one day, have to love in January – that has to love, at least for a time, not "because of" but "in spite of". I said I believed that in every relationship there came a time when at least one of the partners did not "feel" in love – where everything screamed out, "Let go. This is over. Walk away."

I said, "Today you have made vows to each other – vows that dared to enter the joy of this perfect day and warn of darker days. You said, 'I will love you if we are rich', and the vow asked, 'And if you are poor?' You said, 'I will love you for better', and the vow whispered, 'And what of worse?' You said, 'I will love you if you are well', and the vow said, 'Consider sickness too.' "

Will those vows ever be called in for that young couple? As surely as night follows day, they will. Marriages break up, relationships fail – those things are a fact of life. But it's also a fact that we will never find a lasting relationship with anybody unless we are ready at some time to fight to keep our love alive against the odds – to love in January.

I remember counselling a couple in their mid-twenties; they had a baby girl aged six months and were about to divorce. I asked the man why he wanted to divorce his wife. He said, "I don't feel in love anymore."

As he spoke, I couldn't help but gaze at the little bundle that his wife cradled in her arms. I said, "Did nobody tell you when you married that there will be times when the *feeling* of love will diminish? Did nobody warn you that love that lasts does so by loving – at least for a time – with not the heart, but the *will*? Did nobody say that unless you understand this, you are doomed to move from relationship to relationship at the mercy of your feelings?" He looked genuinely surprised. "No," he said. "Nobody told me that."

Nobody told him this and yet grasping this simple principle would allow many relationships that fall at the first hurdle to at least have a chance of surviving. You will not keep your family together if a prerequisite is that you and your partner always feel in love with each other.

Couples that stay together are prepared to go through

periods in their relationship when commitment, responsibility, and sometimes "what's best for the children" is what keeps them together. "For the sake of the kids" is not always the right reason to stay together, but it's still a good reason. None of us wants to live our whole lives loving with gritted teeth, but there are thousands of couples who tried again, perhaps "for the sake of the kids", and in the process found again a love they'd thought was gone forever.

In fact, one major study reported that two-thirds of "unhappy couples" who remained married said they were happy five years later.[10] Some of this is no surprise; the authors of the report suggested that although divorce decreases some areas of stress, it also creates new problems – managing new parenting arrangements, dealing with the reactions of children, financial and health issues, and sometimes in the middle of all this, the challenges that come with establishing a new relationship.

In almost every marriage there will come a time when the "feeling" of love is at a very low ebb. Such times may creep up on us over the years or may be linked to specific strains in the relationship – perhaps following the birth of a child, financial pressure, sickness, or redundancy – when the self-esteem of one of the partners is very low. And it's at this point that something sometimes enters the relationship that, in its ability to destroy families, is in a league of its own: the affair.

The Price Tag Reads...

Some time ago I met Jeremy. He too had reached a period in his marriage when he no longer "felt in love". Whether that was hastened by his being attracted to a woman in his office is something we'll never know. But I suspect his marriage had been going through a stale patch, and the new woman made him look at his wife, his life – his lot – with a growing dissatisfaction.

He told me his story on a rainy Saturday afternoon in a McDonald's next to a cinema complex. He was now divorced and had recently broken up with the woman he'd left his wife for. He had access to his children once every two weeks. Rhys was five and Victoria ten. They were sitting at a nearby table, colouring and looking bored.

He said, "It's hard to know where to take them if it's raining," and then added, "I'd like to tell all the men out there that the affair is great – for a while. The sex is great, and the excitement is great, and the feeling of being young again is great – but it's just not worth it. These are my kids, for goodness' sake. I'm their father and I've just been with them for three hours stuck in a lousy cinema because there's nowhere else to go, and now I have to take them back like a couple of library books."

Over the past twenty years or so, I've seen all kinds of things destroy families. But I believe that nothing comes close to the affair for having the ability so quickly and with such surgical skill to decimate families – and often for so little. It's as if the affair whispers: "Trust me. I know you've heard what this can do to families, but it will be different for you. Just take the next step."

Of course, the end results of the affair can vary. Some people find new and fulfilling relationships, and some feel cheated after just a few days, but in my experience those involved in an affair exhibit the same two characteristics time and time again.

The first is what somebody called "a period of

temporary insanity". During this time, people act totally out of character. They set aside previously held personal or religious beliefs. They sometimes begin to dress differently – perhaps younger, more daring – and almost everything in their lives – children, job, home – comes second to the sheer thrill of this affair.

During this period, people often "rewrite" the story of their lives. They say things such as, "We were so young when we got married – we didn't really know what we were doing", "We've never really been happy", "I was always dissatisfied with our relationship." It's not that they haven't gone through difficult times, but the trick of the affair is that it manages to wipe out every memory of love or happiness that ever genuinely existed.

If that's the first characteristic, then the second always follows – it may come within a few weeks or it could take a few years to happen – but there is no exception. It's a moment when reality kicks in. For a while, everything in the new relationship is thrilling and fun, but eventually the excitement dies and the couple discover that even in their new love nest the taps still leak, the bills still need paying, and babies still wake up crying in the middle of the night. In short, they discover that "the other man's grass may be greener, but it still needs mowing".

The shock of this second stage is often cataclysmic. It's as if at the beginning of the affair the cost was negligible, but that quickly changes. In the early stages, the price is rarely on the ticket – in fact, at the beginning, the price tag reads, "Free". There's no harm in it – some flirting, a little time together. But as it progresses, it's as if there's somebody at the back of the store changing the price ticket – because suddenly it's more expensive. It now calls for a little deceit – "I'll be home a little later on Tuesday, darling." But, hey, even if the price is getting higher, the rewards are fantastic – fun, almost teenage-like conversation, incredible sex. They say to themselves, "This is the person I should have married."

Then one day, they walk into the shop and the price tag has changed for the last time. And now it reads: "*Everything*". They gasp when they see it. They protest that they couldn't possibly pay it without losing almost all they've ever loved – their husband, their wife, their kids, maybe their friends and wider family, and perhaps their home or even their job.

I get angry listening to so-called experts talk about affairs being good for a marriage. Can marriages recover from affairs? Of course. Can those marriages be stronger than they were before? Yes, without doubt. But the affair is a breach of trust so great that it tears at the very heart of a relationship, and although the love may return, it may take a long time for trust to be restored. And affairs are bad for kids.

I know that marriages break up. I know that some marriages cannot survive. I understand that. But the affair is in a class of its own for destroying the world of ordinary families – families that weren't perfect, but could have made it and been relatively happy together. The affair could happen to you and to me tomorrow, so let's consider something George Bernard Shaw said: "There are two great tragedies in life: the one is not to get the desire of your heart; the other is to get it."

We live in a world where personal happiness is put at a premium, but often when we pursue it, we find it eludes us. Sometimes, even for the sake of our own long-term happiness, we have to begin not with what is "best for me", but for *them*.

We have to love – at least for a time – in January.

Action Points

Try to remember the good times – take a trip down Memory Lane with your old photographs.

Don't bring your partner down in front of the kids – even if you're going through a tough time at the moment.

Practise acts of kindness, even when you don't "feel" in love.

Aim to have an evening with your husband or wife at least once a week – defend it with your life.

January love can work with our children as well as a partner – sometimes we have to love our kids when we don't "like" them very much.

"I think a good parent isn't one who makes dinner or helps you with homework because I can do that myself, but a person who is always there for you no matter what and will always love and accept you for who you are."
Thirteen-year-old girl

To Appreciate the Extended Family

My sisters, Val and Joan, never forget my birthday, nor do they forget Dianne's or my children's birthdays. I wish I could tell you that I never forget theirs – and I might be tempted to if I didn't think they'd get hold of a copy of this book. Fortunately for me they still look on me as their kid brother and therefore afford me a latitude I don't deserve. But they are right not to forget – the extended family is important.

Isolated Families

For many people of my generation, we didn't have to try too hard to remember our extended family when we were young – for the very good reason that we saw them most days. Uncles and aunties might live in the same street as us, grandparents just around the corner, and grown-up siblings in the same house. In those days, a young mum didn't have to buy a book on parenting to discover whether it was unusual for her first baby to cry most of the night. She had at least six parenting experts who lived within a half-mile of her – and she was related to all of them.

Today families can easily be spread across the country and even the world. But even if we have to work hard to overcome the geographical barriers, we should at least try to stay in touch. A recent survey found that 53 per cent of people said they don't see their family enough.[11] The truth is that isolation is not good for us. The lack of people with whom to share problems and experiences can leave families without the day-to-day support they need and result in loneliness and frustration. One mum wrote, "I always wish I had my family here and failing that, real friends I can count on. It's a real struggle for me each day to be on top of the issues I face daily as a wife, mother, and employee."

And in addition to the physical isolation that often affects modern families, it could be that our family has a history of hurts and offences. This is not unusual. One man put it like this: "I know that blood is thicker than water. The only problem is, when it comes to my family, most of it is on the carpet."

We may have brothers and sisters we haven't spoken to for years – perhaps after that silly row at the wedding or funeral – but more likely we will have extended family from whom we've just drifted apart. If possible, we should try to mend those fences – swallow a little pride and make that phone call.

The extended family is important for our children. It's good for them to have an understanding of not just the "roots" of our family but the "branches", and the wider family can also give them a strong sense of belonging and therefore security. And for a child it makes a huge difference to know there are people outside the immediate family who really care about you.

The Generation Game

Perhaps a good place to start is with a child's grandparents. Now, this would surely be easier if all grandparents fitted the storybook image. It wouldn't be hard to visit the old lady with round, silver-framed spectacles who bakes her own bread and wipes her hands on her apron while telling the kids stories. But in the modern world, Gran might be quite different. She may be a successful career woman just reaching the top of her game, or busy going out each day loving her new-found freedom from responsibility for children. And Granddad may have decided that the pipe and slippers image doesn't suit him and has taken up karate instead.

But if it's true that life in modern families can sometimes be more complicated than in previous generations, it's also true that most grandparents desperately want to be involved in their grandchildren's lives. And in a world where so many people – especially young people – feel insecure and somewhat disconnected, children *need* their grandparents.

There's a line in an African song: "When an old person dies, it's as if a library burns down." Your children's grandparents often hold the keys to that library – the knowledge of your family's history. Perhaps that's why in societies in which family life is strong, the elderly are listened to; they're allowed to tell the stories of their life to the young, and they are honoured. That doesn't mean they are always pleasant – the kind of folk you can't wait to go on holiday with. But it does mean there's a recognition that they play an important part in the task of helping children take their place in society.

The fact is that the values we pass on to our children are not only taught – but *caught*. The scary thing is not that our children aren't listening to us – but that they *are*. And *watching*. It follows then that the attitudes our children have towards their grandparents (and, rather more frighteningly, the attitudes they may have towards us when we're older) will be moulded to some extent by the attitudes we model. If we're too busy to write to, visit – even telephone – our parents, then why should a teenager take the time to go to see Gran? But if we "honour" our older family members – speak well of them in front of our children, listen to their stories of younger days, and let the kids overhear us asking them for advice – we'll sow seeds in our children's lives that help them connect to their grandparents.

I can imagine what some of you are saying: "That's all very well, but you don't know how difficult my mother, and particularly my husband's father, is." Perhaps not. But I do think it's worth trying hard in this area. It's not at all impossible for your child to have a good relationship with their grandmother, even though you can't get on with her as a mother-in-law.

As much as possible, try to give your parents quality time with their grandchildren. Not all grandparents come out of the same mould; some take to this new role easily, but with others we may need a little more patience. Some grandparents will love being asked to babysit, while others will be more reticent. If your need for a babysitter and your parents' need to see the kids meet, that's perfect – but don't take it for granted. Talk about expectations with your parents and find a level of contact that works for everyone. Of course, relationships with one set of grandparents may become much harder after a marriage breakdown, but despite the difficulties, it's worth trying hard to keep that connection.

Bill Cosby said, "Grandchildren are God's reward for not killing your kids." I'm pretty sure that's not true, but I do know that the role of grandparent is a vitally important one in the life of a child. And I urge you to help build as strong a relationship as possible between your children and their grandparents.

Of course, sometimes children are separated by long distances from their grandparents, so here are a few ideas to help build a good relationship across the miles:

1. Ask your parents to record stories for your kids that you can play to them. It could be an event from their life or a story from one of your child's favourite books.

2. Put pictures of their grandparents around – on a low shelf for younger children – so they can get used to how they look. It'll make it easier for them when they visit.

3. Ask the grandparents to make a photo album that includes pictures of their surroundings – home, work, hobbies, pets. It will help your child to feel they "know" them.

4. With younger children, send their artwork to your parents and ask them to send back a photograph of it on display in their home.

5. Ask your parents to send notes or postcards to
   your children now and again.

One of my favourite poems was written by a nine-year-old girl. She manages to capture the precious gift that many grandparents are able to give their grandchildren. Here's a short extract:

> Grandmothers don't talk baby talk to us like
>   visitors do,
> because they know it's hard for us
>   to understand it.
> When they read to us, they don't skip pages,
> or mind if it's the same story over and over
>   again.
> Everybody should try to have one,
> especially if you don't have television,
>   ... because grandmas are the only
>   grown-ups who have got time.

Meet the Parents!

But now, just as we've finished considering rosy-cheeked grandparents and think it might be safe to enter the waters of the extended family, a character enters who is vilified by comedians, parodied in pantomimes, and possesses the ability to make grown men and women cry: the in-law.

Of course, many couples have brilliant relationships with their in-laws, but it's not hard to see why this particular dynamic can sometimes be a little challenging. For the parent, it involves that most difficult of parental tasks – letting go of their son or daughter. And for the child, it means the tricky business of – *actually leaving*. So before we go any further, allow me to make a brief comment in defence of the in-law: often, "problems with in-laws" are nothing of the sort. They are "problems with our marriage".

The reason I know this is because early in my own marriage I made some bad mistakes. For years, Dianne and I described certain issues as "problems with in-laws" when they were in fact "problems with our relationship" – in particular, with *me*.

Let me explain. I was close to my mum. She never passed an academic examination, but she was one of the wisest women I've ever known. And boy could she love: she loved us kids with a passion. And as much as I hate to say it, she had a soft spot for me, the youngest. If you don't believe me, ask my older sisters. My mother has been dead for almost ten years, but even now they'd be scared to beat me in a board game in case she was still watching.

I loved my mother. But I foolishly mistook what that love demanded of me. I knew she missed me after I got married so I tried hard to soften that blow. I used to slip in to see her most days – without telling Dianne. I would sometimes share things with her – that I'd not told Dianne. And yes, sometimes my mother was less than wise in letting it show that she felt Dianne's care of "her boy" wasn't quite up to her own standards. But without doubt, the real problem wasn't with my mother but with *me*. In the early years of our marriage, it was as if I were "married" to two women.

I should have taken some advice from what my mother used to call "The Good Book". It says that a man must leave his mother and his father and be joined to his wife. Unless you "leave" – not just physically, but *emotionally* – you can never be really "joined". When I learned that lesson and began to put Dianne *first* in my life, I actually did a better job of caring for my mother too.

But having defended in-laws a little, let's consider for a moment some of the challenges they pose. I remember a woman telling me that when she got married, she struggled to build a good relationship with her mother-in-law. One day she had the idea of asking her mother-in-law for some advice, thinking it might help them bond together. She said, "Carole, have you any tips to stop milk boiling over?" Her mother-in-law answered in a heartbeat. She said, "I've never had milk boil over."

It must be hard having a "perfect" in-law, but even if they don't have that problem, many couples talk to me about in-laws who put pressure on their marriages. One young woman described the effect her father-in-law was having on her marriage as "suffocating". That wasn't a bad choice of word because although the intentions of in-laws are often good, the effects of their actions sometimes make it hard for a marriage to breathe.

That "suffocation" can show itself in many ways: it could be by the continual giving of advice – on parenting, gardening, cooking, or decorating – or constantly and without warning, "dropping in" for a "quick cup of coffee". Some in-laws cannot stop themselves talking to their children about how useless their children's partners are – how they should be getting their wife to "shape up" or their husband to "do something about that pathetic job he's got". Although these parents often justify their involvement to themselves by saying it's for their children's good, they're sometimes driving a stake through the heart of those children's marriages. This is especially so if their children are anxious to please them.

All this would be easier to deal with if we didn't actually care for our adult children, but most parents-in-law want the very best for their children and son-in-law or daughter-in-law. The problem comes when we just can't stop ourselves interfering.

Of course, as I mentioned with my own situation, in-law problems are often not just the fault of the in-laws. Sometimes a husband or wife also tries to go on living after marriage as though nothing has changed. We may still turn too quickly to our parents for emotional support, rather than persevere in finding it from our partner. We may betray the confidences of our marriage by revealing to our parents every row or disappointment we have with our husband or wife or perhaps rush back to our parents every time we have a falling out.

And even as we're doing this, our partner is feeling more and more isolated – as if they're a "spare part" or married to not just their husband or wife, but to their in-laws. I have some respect for the mother whose son turned up on her doorstep six months after he'd got married. "We've had a row," he said. "I'm going to sleep at your place tonight." She replied, "No you're not. Get straight back home and sleep on the couch until you sort it out. You're married now."

In my experience, in-law problems fall broadly into two categories. The first is where the in-laws may be interfering, annoying, and sometimes downright rude, but basically want the best for their child and their son-

or daughter-in-law. They want the marriage to work. In this scenario, I'd encourage couples to be as forgiving and generous as possible towards their in-laws. Smile when you feel like screaming, and when you go home, laugh together. It may well be that you'll need to talk with them about the more serious issues, but first discuss it thoroughly with each other and decide together how you will handle it. And there's the secret – you can get through a lot as long as you are *together* in it and committed to each other before anybody else.

Let's face it – it's possible for in-laws to be downright difficult. But it's also the case that we can sometimes misunderstand them, as Stephanie discovered.[12] She said, "My mother-in-law, Lois, doesn't approve of me or the way I do anything. Last time Joe and I visited her, I washed up the pots and pans after dinner. I left the kitchen but when I went in a few minutes later, I found her washing them all over again!"

Stephanie eventually shared how she felt with Connie, Joe's older sister. She said, "I know your mother hates me and thinks I'm a slob."

Connie was horrified. "Stephanie, it's not about you. It's about Mum's compulsion to have everything spotless. I grew up with her – she was like this before you and Joe even met. When she re-washes things, she's not condemning you. It's simply that she's got different – what most would consider absurd – standards of what's acceptably clean. Let it go. There are bigger hills to die on."

That short conversation had a remarkable effect on the way Stephanie looked at her mother-in-law. They were by no means close, but as she became more understanding, the relationship slowly began to improve.

But as I said, there are two main categories of problems with in-laws, and if the first is with parents who are misguided but want their child's marriage to succeed, the second is with those who actually want to destroy their child's marriage. This is very rare but not unknown. It's probable they never approved of the marriage to begin with.

In this situation, someone needs to talk to the parents, and the person to do it is probably not the son- or daughter-in-law, but the son or daughter themselves. And it's absolutely vital that you, as a couple, stay together in this. Your marriage is in danger – and you are fighting *together* to keep it alive.

Time's Great Trick

Of course, family life moves on, and it may be that the difficult in-law, or the grandfather who loved to tell your children stories and make them laugh by taking his teeth out, has become the parent that you now have to care for.

My mother-in-law, Anne, has Alzheimer's disease. When I visit her with Dianne, I watch the interaction between them. As soon as Dianne enters the room, this old lady's face lights up. Dianne used to say, "Do you remember my name?" But too many disappointments have stopped her asking that question. Instead she'll say, "You look pretty today" or "You've got your new cardigan on."

There will be some minutes when Anne just talks. It's true there will be moments of clarity, but for the most part it will be a jumble of gentle nonsense until Dianne interrupts and says, "What shall we do today?" In truth,

Anne will never leave her room again, but one advantage of her confused mind is that almost anything is possible, and soon a mother and her daughter are planning a shopping trip.

"Shall we take the bus or go by car?" asks Dianne.

"Oh!" shrieks Anne. "The bus!"

"And what do we need to get?" says Dianne, reaching for a pen and paper. I smile as I watch an old lady, who once ran a large office, dictate a list so fast that Dianne (now her junior secretary!) can hardly keep up. But there is never a demand to see it all through – to catch the bus, to browse the shelves of the department store. It's as if, in her very heart, she *knows*. She knows that just as she played shops with the woman sitting beside her when that woman was a child, so now they are playing the old game again.

But now it's time to eat, and I watch as Dianne lifts the spoon of soup to Anne's lips and wipes a little spillage off the new cardigan. Eventually it's time to go and Dianne tucks the bedclothes in around her mother and whispers, "Shall we say prayers together?"

And suddenly I know what is happening. Time has performed its great trick: the mother has become the daughter and the daughter the mother.

These experiences are common to many of us, and this can be such a difficult time. Couples in this situation are sometimes called "the sandwich generation" – caring for their own children, perhaps even their grandchildren, and at the same time caring for elderly parents.

It can be a time of incredible pressure, having to decide what's best for elderly relatives and trying to cope with the ever-present guilt of making what we fear could be a wrong decision. This is how one man put it:

> People have no idea of the guilt involved in trying to do your best for somebody you love with all your heart. My mum is very ill – she needs skilled nursing care – somebody to be there twenty-four hours a day. I know that I can't provide that for her, yet every time I enter the nursing home the guilt almost chokes me.

At such times the whole family needs to be there for each other – to lay down past squabbles, to seek advice from others, to work out what is best together, and to support each other in the decisions taken.

Perhaps the phrase "to support each other" sums up part of what family life is all about. Brothers, sisters, uncles, aunties, nephews, nieces, grandparents, and in-laws – they may not be the ones we would have picked had we been given a choice, but they're all the family we've got.

It's not always possible, but try hard to keep connected to this extended family – and remember that a "My, how you've grown" and a powdery kiss from an ancient auntie never did any kid any harm.

Action Points

Let your children talk to their grandparents on the telephone. Even if your child is too young to talk, let them listen to Granddad's voice on the phone.

Encourage your parents to tell stories from "the old days". Even though we may be bored of them, to our kids they are often magical.

Build as strong a relationship with your in-laws as possible, but remember that respecting them doesn't entail obeying all their parental requests.

Go easy on criticizing your in-laws to your husband or wife – they know more negative things about their parents than you do but they may still not appreciate hearing about them from you.

Protect your own marriage – be a team in the way you deal with your extended family.

Trace your family's history – maybe prepare a family tree – and allow your children to see their place in your family story.

Ask your parents to take your children on a tour of their lives – showing them the houses they lived in, the school they went to, and places that have significance for them.

Try to re-establish links that have been broken in your

extended family. You don't have to try to change the world – just a note or a phone call.

For help in dealing with the issue of caring for elderly relatives in the UK, visit www.careforthefamily.org.uk/supportnet

Life Lesson 10:

To Seize the Moment

Our time together is almost over, and since we met those brand new parents in the hospital car park we've talked about a lot: making time for our family and planning it in; discovering the power of encouragement; January love; why acceptance is vital if we are to believe we are loved; and much more. But I'm very conscious that there will be some readers who are, at this moment, going through a very difficult time in their family – so much so you feel like giving up.

I work with Care for the Family, a UK charity. We provide support for families in all kinds of situations, including stepfamilies and single parent families, and help and counsel for parents who have children with additional needs. We try to help those who have been widowed early in life, as well as getting alongside families in the ordinary issues of marriage and parenting that affect most homes. This experience has convinced me of two things. First, there are no easy answers to the traumas of family life. And second, the primary need that most of us have is not for "answers", but to know that we are not alone. What keeps us going in the tough times is hope: the belief that because others have come through experiences like ours – we can too.

Another area in which we work is supporting parents who have experienced the death of a child – it could be through accident, illness, or sometimes murder. This is a devastating event for families on so many levels. In addition to dealing with the grief of losing their child and at a time when they need each other most, many couples also experience tremendous strains in their own relationship.

Each of the "Befrienders", who offer support to parents, has lost a child themselves. The other day, as I was talking to one of them – Peter – I heard an incredible example of how discovering you're not alone can be life changing. I asked him how things had gone on the previous weekend's conference for bereaved parents. This is what he said:

"On the Friday afternoon when the parents arrived, I could tell that some – particularly the men – just didn't want to be there. They sat with their arms folded as if saying, 'We shouldn't have come. This will be a waste of time. You can't give us our child back.'

"And then I told them how our son died, aged twenty-one. How, though my wife and I love each other, she couldn't get near me. I'd just walk and cry. I didn't want to take my life, but I didn't want to live either. Sometimes people would say, 'Peter, time will heal.' But it doesn't heal. The pain gets easier, but it doesn't heal – it's not meant to. And I told them how one person had said to me, 'But, Peter, you've got three other great children.' And I'd said, 'I know, but I want *him*.'"

He went on, "Sharing our story and being honest with people has an incredible effect. By Sunday afternoon it was as if these grieving parents had opened up like flowers – one man just sidled up to me and whispered, 'Thank you.' And it's not that we gave them answers – there are no easy answers. We just gave them an understanding that others have walked, and are walking, this path – and coming through it."

It's very hard to deal with difficult times in family life unless we are given hope from others who have come through similar times. This is true not just in parenting, but in marriage. Time and time again I've talked with couples where one of the parties had believed there was no way forward except to leave the relationship. But before that actually happened, they'd got the opportunity to talk to somebody about the situation – perhaps a counsellor or another couple who'd come through a similar time themselves. They'd decided to have another go at making their relationship work, and years later they often say something like this: "We are so glad we tried again. It seemed so definitely right to split up, but now we've got a relationship we would have thought impossible five years ago. And we still have our family together."

Being able to share with friends, colleagues, and even counsellors, can be an incredible help in getting us through some of the difficult times that hit our families. And perhaps the sooner we stop pretending, or bowing to the pressure to have the "perfect family", we'll find that we're able to support each other more effectively. The truth is we're all trying to get through as best we can.

A mother once wrote to me and said, "If I ever leave my family, it will surely be at a quarter past five." Mothers all over the world understand why she'd say that. It's the time of day when you're standing in the kitchen surrounded by mayhem: the two youngest kids are squabbling over what to watch on the television; the fish fingers are burned; the hamster has just escaped down the small hole behind the sink; the boss has just rung to ask whether you intended to get that report in today; your fourteen-year-old has just declared he's giving up maths "because it's rubbish"; and you've just discovered that the frozen chips aren't frozen – and neither is anything else, actually – because last night somebody left the freezer door open.

But in fact, most mothers *don't* leave then because they've been through hundreds of "quarter past fives" before and they've learned that these times pass. The other day, I had an anonymous note from a mother of teenagers. She said, "I don't like being a parent anymore. It's very hard and I don't have the energy." I felt moved as I read it because I believe she probably thinks she's the only mother on the face of the earth who feels that way – and she therefore feels a failure.

But the truth is that many parents have felt, and are feeling, this way. It's common for the parents of teenagers to feel like failures – to say, "Where did we go wrong?" and "I'm not sure I can cope anymore." Actually, most of us are doing a much better job of parenting than we think – and it normally turns out better than we dared hope. Grunting teenagers discover language sooner or later, and most untidy kids get fed up with living in a toxic zone. And when they find a job they really want to

114

do, most of them get off their bottoms and give it their best shot. I wish I could find the mother who wrote that note and get the chance to say, "It's not just you. Don't give up – not even inside."

"I'll Be Happy When..."

Perhaps it's because family life can often be filled with stresses – major and minor – that it's easy to fall into the trap of wishing away the current period of our family life. We say, "Life will be easier... when the baby's sleeping through the night/the kids start nursery" or perhaps, if we're naïve, "When the children become teenagers, they'll need less attention." A psychologist friend of mine said to me one day, "Most people believe a future event will make them happy. They say, 'When I get married I'll be happy' or 'When we have children...' or 'When I get a new job...' or even something insignificant like, 'When the weekend comes – then I'll be happy.'" Then he said, "But really happy people don't think about their lives like that – even though life may be far from perfect, they learn to appreciate the good bits. They grasp happiness – however small – *now*."

I think we can do that more easily if we realize how fast the stages of family life pass. I remember thinking when my children were small that the years ahead seemed like the start of the long summer holiday when we were kids – practically eternal. But then somebody suggested imagining that an egg timer contained not sand but days. It's sobering. When your child is born, the timer has 6,570 days in it – the number of days until they reach eighteen. If your child is ten years old, 3,650 days have already gone – you have 2,920 left. No amount of money, power, or prestige can increase that number by a single day.

I know of no better way to convince you of the speed with which family life passes than to share a story I came across many years ago. It concerns a man in his late mid-life who did a little maths one day. He knew that the average age to which he might live was seventy-five years. He then multiplied that by fifty-two to give him a figure of 2,800 – the number of Saturdays his life would hold. But he was already fifty-five and therefore had just 1,000 Saturdays left.

He went straight out and toured the toy shops in his local town until he managed to buy a thousand marbles. When he got home, he put them all in a large jar – each of them representing one of the Saturdays he had left in life. And in the days, months, and years ahead he took out a marble each week.

One day he was speaking to a younger man who was finding it hard in his busy schedule to find enough time for his wife and children. He told the younger man about the marbles and said, "Watching the marbles diminish helped me to focus on the really important things in life." Then he went to fetch the jar. When he returned, the young man could see that the jar was empty. The older man said, "Today I am seventy-five, so just before I took my lovely wife out for breakfast this morning, I took out the last marble. Any Saturdays from now on are a bonus."

We need our family. It's the place where we discover who we are – our gifts and ambitions, our hopes and fears. It's the small body of people who help us prepare to face a whole world, to learn what works and what doesn't.

And ultimately, if it works well, our family are those who will be there for us not because they think we're special, but because we are part of *them*. One thirteen-year-old girl put it like this:

> A family should trust each other and be nothing but themselves when around each other. A good family is not the perfect family like shown on TV, but the family that is happy overall and can help each other through bad times.[13]

But what of that young couple in the car park? What does the future hold for them and the little bundle they now so gingerly load into the back of their car? And what does it hold for us? The truth is that whatever it holds, we'll face it more easily if we're able to do that as part of a strong family. Perhaps all of us can realize afresh that families are important and, if possible – even where there's been hurt – at least try to sustain our relationships: make that call to a sister; write a letter to that brother; don't lose heart with the teenager who's driving you crazy; reach out to that estranged child; don't take your husband or wife for granted – and if you have lost a love you once had for each other, perhaps try once more to rediscover it.

With all its joys, pains, fears, and hopes...

... this is your family.

References

1 Rob Parsons, *The Sixty Minute Father*, Hodder & Stoughton, 2009.

2 Christopher Lasch, *Haven in a Heartless World: The Family Beseiged*, W. W. Norton & Co, new edition, 1995.

3 A. Sacker, I. Schoon, and M. Bartley, "Social inequality in educational achievement and psychosocial adjustment throughout childhood: magnitude and mechanisms", *Social Science and Medicine*, v.55 n.5, pp. 863–880, 2002.

4 Stephen R. Covey, *The 7 Habits of Highly Effective Families*, B Jain Publishers Pvt Ltd, new edition, 2006.

5 Barbara L. Fredrickson and Marcial F. Losada, "Positive Affect and the Complex Dynamics of Human Flourishing", *American Psychologist*, v.60 n.7, pp. 678–686, October 2005.

6 Larissa Pople, *The Good Childhood Inquiry. Family: A summary of themes emerging from children and young people's evidence*, The Children's Society, 2009.

7 Stephen R. Covey, *The 7 Habits of Highly Effective Families*, B Jain Publishers Pvt Ltd, new edition, 2006.

8 Marianne M. Jennings, "Kitchen Table Vital to Family Life", *Deseret News*, 9 February 1997.

9 Anne Garvey, "When the Children Leave Home...", *Guardian*, 5 March 2003.

10 L. Waite et al., *Does Divorce Make People Happy? Findings from a Study of Unhappy Marriages*, IAV, 2002.

11 www.netmums.com/campaigns/A_Mum_s_Life.656

12 David & Claudia Arp and John & Margaret Bell, *Loving Your Relatives*, Tyndale House Publishers, 2003.

13 Larissa Pople, *The Good Childhood Inquiry. Family: A summary of themes emerging from children and young people's evidence*, The Children's Society, 2009.

Afterword

Rob Parsons
Founder and Executive Chairman
of Care for the Family

Introducing Care for the Family

I hope that you've enjoyed this book and feel that you have gained some practical help and insight that will strengthen and enrich your family life!

At Care for the Family we are committed to providing support that strengthens family life and helps those who are hurting because of family difficulty. Over the past twenty-one years, hundreds of thousands of people have attended our events and our staff of over a hundred supports single parents, those parenting children with additional needs, bereaved parents, and a host of other family situations.

When I helped found the charity in 1988, it was because I believed that it was important for families to be cared for. We work hard to produce world-class resources to help families and are keen to know if what we provide makes a difference.

Please let us know whether you found this book helpful by going to www.careforthefamily. org.uk/survey/family where you can complete a short survey and send us your views. We look forward to hearing from you!

If you are ever facing a difficult family situation, or are looking for ways to make your family relationships even stronger, then give us a call on **+44 (0) 29 2081 0800**. Much more information – including articles and advice – is available online at www.careforthefamily.org.uk.

And remember Care for the Family is *your* family charity. We are always there for you.

With very best wishes,

21st Century Parent

Eight short talks by Rob Parsons to inspire and encourage every parent – with a helpful hints booklet full of discussion starters, top tips and ideas for action.

Parents often feel caught between the pressures of today and worries about tomorrow. But you can build strong relationships with your children today that will help steer them towards **a fulfilling life**.

£12.99
complete with booklet

For over 20 years, Rob Parsons has encouraged thousands of parents to forge stronger relationships with their children and become the best parents they can be. Here he shares some lessons he's learned as a parent – and some mistakes he's made along the way, too.

Topics include:
- You're not alone
- The testing child
- Do what you can
- Teenagers!
- The gift of acceptance
- A mother looks back (with Dianne Parsons)
- Building a sense of value
- Defending the boundaries

You can use 21st Century Parent to help strengthen your family – and families you know. The DVD comes with a helpful hints booklet full of discussion starters, top tips and ideas for action.

320-09 A

Order today at www.careforthefamily.org.uk/21cfamily or phone (029) 2081 0800

21st Century Marriage

Long-lasting, happy marriages don't just happen – they need looking after. In the 21st century the pressures on relationships are greater than ever and sometimes we need a bit of extra help.

For over 20 years, Rob Parsons has helped thousands of couples build stronger relationships.
In this compelling DVD, through eight short talks, Rob lifts the lid on what can make or break those relationships.

£12.99 complete with booklet

21st Century Marriage covers:
- The power of acceptance
- Dealing with debt
- Sex and intimacy
- When sparks fly
- Time pressure
- Love in the real world

21st Century Marriage is ideal for couples, but can also be used with small groups. The DVD comes with a helpful hints booklet full of discussion starters, top tips and ideas for action.

320-09 D